Y17662

Enfield Highway
Library
Hertford Road
Enfield 443-2300

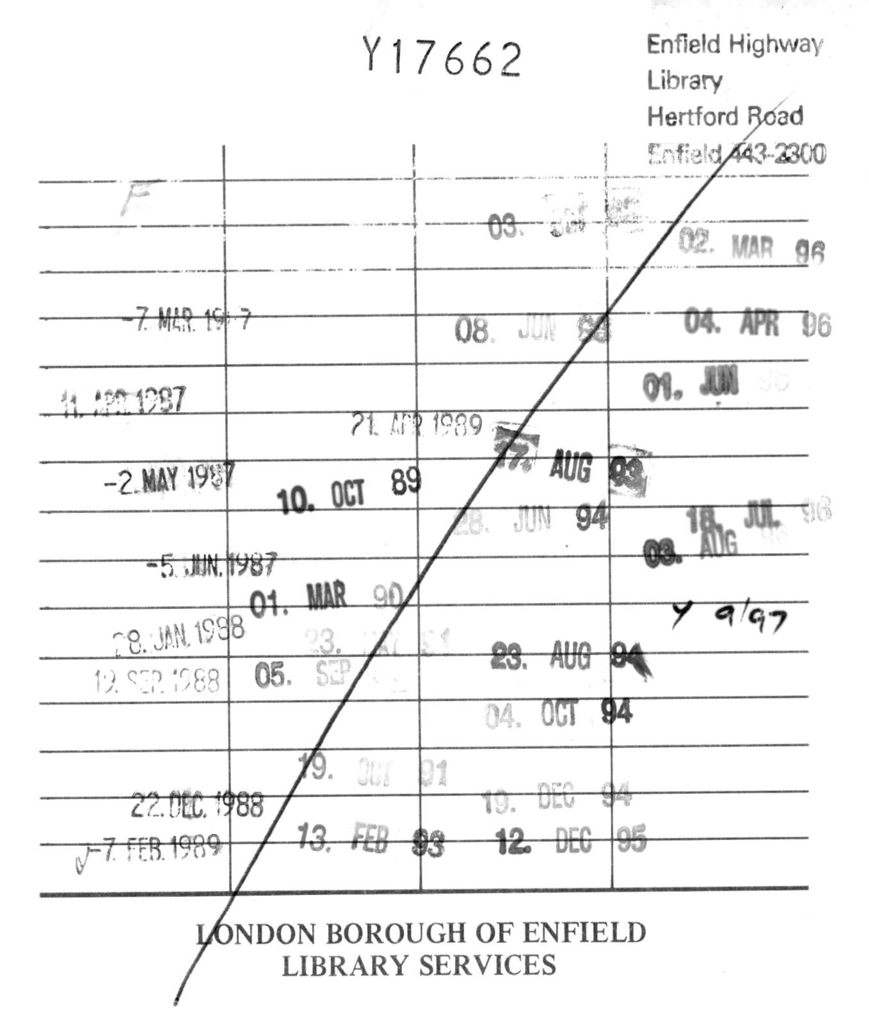

LONDON BOROUGH OF ENFIELD
LIBRARY SERVICES

This book to be RETURNED on or before the latest date stamped unless a renewal has been obtained by personal call or post, quoting the above number and the date due for return.

Enfield Highwa
Library
Hertford Road
Enfield 443-230(

BY THE SAME AUTHOR

The Teachers (ISBN 0 903214 05 9)
Eastland Press

NORTH SEA SURGE

The story of the East Coast Floods of 1953

by

MICHAEL POLLARD

Enfield Highway
Library
Hertford Road
Enfield 443-2300

TERENCE DALTON LIMITED
LAVENHAM . SUFFOLK
1978

Published in the United Kingdom by
TERENCE DALTON LIMITED
ISBN 0 86138 021 5

First published 1978
Second impression 1982

London Borough
of Enfield
Public Libraries
Y17662
942·6

Text photoset in 11/12pt Baskerville

Printed in Great Britain by
THE LAVENHAM PRESS LIMITED
LAVENHAM . SUFFOLK

© Michael Pollard 1978

Contents

Introduction 8

Chapter One 11

Chapter Two 30

Chapter Three 51

Chapter Four 70

Chapter Five 93

Chapter Six 109

Acknowledgements 130

Index 133

Index of Illustrations

Passable by boat only ... 7
Rescuer and rescued ... 10
Breach at Overy Staithe ... 13
Bank after the flood... ... 14
Coastguard at Lowestoft ... 17
Weather, noon 30th January 1953 18
Weather, 06.00 31st January 1953 21
Weather, 06.00 1st February 1953 23
Aerial view of floods Spurn Head 26
Damage at Mablethorpe ... 29
The quay at Wells 31
Tipper lorry 33
Wrecked bungalow at Snettisham... 35
Mrs Beckerton shows injuries 37
Survivors at rest centre ... 39
Marooned train 41
Felixstowe prefab site ... 43
Mrs Beckerton and children 46
U.S. servicemen in Norfolk... 50
Ferry Road area, Southwold 52
Slaughden, near Aldeburgh 54
Felixstowe seafront 56
Main Road, Harwich ... 58
Rescue by boat in Harwich... 59
Albert Street, Harwich ... 60
The front at Dovercourt ... 61
Jaywick Sunday morning ... 63
Bomber all at sea in Essex ... 65
Canvey Island, Monday morning 66
Calling and listening ... 67
Boat rescue of islanders ... 69
Aerial survey 71
Canvey's police check ... 72
Servicemen on Canvey Island 74
Collecting drowned sheep ... 76
The Queen at Snettisham ... 78
Sunday at Burnham Overy Town 80
Evacuation of Canvey Island 82
Civilian labour 84
Armed forces work force ... 85
Sandbag air drop 86
Rescue and relief at Harwich 89
Survivor carried to safety ... 92
Clothing for victims 94
Red Cross canteen 95
Caravans for flood homeless 97
Repair at Burnham Overy Staithe 98
Rescue of terrified pig ... 101
Scene at Mablethorpe ... 104
Flood water inland 107
Refugees from Canvey Island 108
Rescue at Kings Lynn ... 111
Rest centre for survivors ... 114
Humour in adversity ... 117
Night sandbagging 118
Wave wall 119
Dune erosion 120
Sand and the wave wall ... 122
Road to the sea 123
Beach bungalow at Heacham 124
Inn at Sea Palling 125
Heacham caravan site ... 126
New development, Hunstanton 127
Could it happen again? ... 129

Cley, on the north Norfolk coast – and the High Street is passable for boats only.
Press Association

Introduction

THE NIGHT of Saturday, 31st January 1953, brought to Britain one of the greatest peacetime disasters in her history.

As darkness fell, fierce gales were raging over the whole country, but this is not unusual in late January. From the Meteorological Office, then based at Dunstable, routine gale warnings had been issued, but even among the experts there was no suspicion of what the night might bring. And although trees creaked and occasionally fell, tiles were torn from roofs and, on the coast, boats began to snatch uneasily at their moorings, there was no reason at all why the villagers of Sea Palling in Norfolk should not get themselves ready for their regular whist drive, or why the members and friends of the Lowestoft Choral Society should not dress up for their annual dinner at the Suffolk Hotel, or why an American service family living at Felixstowe should not have some friends over from the Bentwaters air base for a convivial evening. Indeed, there is something particularly appealing about such occasions on a wild night.

The night was wild all right. When it was over, more than 300 people had been drowned, along with thousands of cattle, pigs, sheep and poultry. Over 40,000 people had been evacuated from their homes, with many thousands more still waiting for rescue, and over 150,000 acres of land had been flooded—much of it prime agricultural land which had been rendered sterile for a season or more. From Lincolnshire to Kent, long stretches of Britain's most vulnerable coastline had been made unrecognisable.

It was the night of the great flood, a night that lives in the memories of the people of the east coast as vividly as do the nights of the Blitz in the memories of Londoners. "Nightmare", appropriately enough, is a word they often use when they talk about it—and nightmare it certainly was as green seas pursued them inexorably up their staircases or, more disastrously, swept in upon them in their bedrooms. Many East Anglian families, and not only those which lost loved ones, are still psychologically marred by the disaster. For some, there are occasional physical reminders, as on one Norfolk farm where the plough still, nearly twenty-five years later, occasionally turns up pots of ink, bottles, combs and other items from a village shop which was literally dashed to pieces by the sea. "People tell me I am silly and that I should forget," writes one survivor. "But how can I sweep from my mind that awful huge wave that engulfed our home? I still re-live it whenever we have a heavy storm." A continuing souvenir for thousands of home-owners in the coastal towns and villages is the difficulty of decorating walls which were saturated with sea-water and will, according to expert advice, never again take and hold paint or paper satisfactorily.

My original plan for this book was to tell the full story of the 1953 disaster, minute by minute — an ambition which was soon dashed when I found that a book of 800-plus pages had been written about events in one county alone. It soon became clear, too, that the fund of reminiscences among the people of the areas concerned was so rich that anything other than a selection of their stories would be repetitive and unmanageable. The compromise I have adopted is to set just some of these accounts in the context of a more generalised story of the night's events and their aftermath. This, I hope, gives a reasonably balanced picture if by no means an exhaustive one.

This, then, is the story of just a few of the people who — physically, at least — survived that night. It is a characteristic of experiences of this kind that they generate their own folklore. Thus one feature of the East Anglian stories is the miraculous survival of pigs, a species which, on that night's showing, seems to rival the cat as a born survivor, some floating about on sofas until they were rescued and one finding itself marooned in a pig's paradise — a potato clamp which provided both food and, when it burrowed down to the straw, a bed. The night of the flood brought its humorous moments as well as its overwhelmingly tragic ones. The rescued parrot of Harwich became a legend in its own time, as did the motorist on the Dovercourt road who, seeing a line of multicoloured Trinity House buoys flagging him down, leapt from his car and ran as fast as he could in the opposite direction.

But in the main this is, like accounts of all such times of tragedy, a testimony to the fact that in times of stress there is in people — the feckless, the stand-offish, the self-seeking and the self-centred along with the rest — a reservoir of courage and selflessness which, unfortunately, is brought out only under the levelling circumstances of disaster.

The individuals, organisations and publications to whom my thanks are due are listed at the back of the book. I should, however, make it clear that the comments on the reaction to the disaster of the government of the day, and on the possibility of a recurrence, are my own except where otherwise directly attributed.

Michael Pollard
Burnham Norton, 1977

A picture that tells it all: the indomitable cheerfulness of the rescuers, the bewilderment and fear of the rescued. *Press Association*

CHAPTER ONE

ENGLAND'S eastern coastline,* and in particular the coast of Norfolk and Suffolk, is especially vulnerable to the sea. As fishermen have known for centuries, and oilmen have discovered more recently, the North Sea is, at the best of times, a moody and challenging stretch of water, and after the "weather window" closes with the beginning of autumn it becomes, for six months, wild and unpredictable. The tides funnel southwards, entering the North Sea between Scotland and Norway and bearing down on the neck of water between East Anglia and the Netherlands, constricted as they flow, until they meet the secondary Atlantic tides which have made their way up the English Channel. The balance between land and sea on the southern shores of the North Sea is a fine one, and there are few winters in which some damage is not caused, whether by the encroachment of flood water on low-lying land or by the collapse of stretches of cliff.

Most of the eastern coast is flat and low-lying. The occasional stretches of cliff—for example, between Weybourne and Happisburgh on the north-eastern tip of Norfolk and, further round the coast, in brief outcrops between Caister and Brightlingsea—are of boulder clay which yields readily to the attacks of the sea. Indeed, in normal conditions the action of the sea poses more of a threat to clifftop settlements than to low-lying areas. Cromer, for instance, has always suffered badly. William White's *History of Norfolk*, published in 1845, noted that the wreckage off Cromer included Shipden, "a considerable village which, with its church, dedicated to St Peter, appears to have been swallowed by the sea about the time of Henry IV", together with "more than twenty houses (which) have been ingulfed in the memory of some of the present inhabitants". There were further heavy cliff falls in the area in 1799, 1825 and 1845. Attempts by Cromer residents to establish a more secure trading community on the sea-front were dogged, throughout the nineteenth century, by tidal mishaps. An extraordinarily high tide in February 1836, says White, washed away Mr S. Simons' Bath House "with a man in it", and "so shattered Mr Randell's Warm Baths on the beach that he removed them into Jetty Street". Two breakwaters were washed away—in 1822 and 1845—with the result that property-owners near the sea were rated at twenty shillings in the pound, a fairly punitive rate for those days, for new sea defence works.

The flat coastlands which make up most of the eastern seaboard are defended from the sea by natural or man-made barriers which protect the land—some of it below sea-level—behind. Centuries of struggle have given

*For the purpose of this book designated as that part of the east coast of England which lies south of the Humber.

landowners and, more recently, public authorities plenty of experience in the defence of the land against the incursions of the sea. But it has always been a fight—and often one that the land has lost. Successive batterings and scourings have claimed, for example, the numerous churches of the once substantial town of Dunwich, which, although virtually destroyed by the sixteenth century, continued to return a Member of Parliament until 1832, when the constituency was abolished as a "rotten borough"—one of three on the East Anglian coast. The old church of Walton-on-the-Naze, too, lies some way out under the North Sea. The abbots of Barking, who owned large tracts of land bordering the Thames Estuary, fought a wearisome battle throughout the Middle Ages in an attempt to prevent their reclaimed grazing land from turning back into saltings. And there were human casualties, too. In December 1287, nearly two hundred people were drowned at Hickling, in Norfolk, when the sea broke through in the middle of the night and, according to a contemporary account, "suffocated or drowned men and women sleeping in their beds, with infants in their cradles, and all kinds of cattle and fresh-water fishes. Many, when surrounded by the waters, sought a place of refuge by mounting into trees; but benumbed by the cold, they were overtaken by the water and fell into it and were drowned".

Not all was loss, however. It has been calculated that since Tudor times, taking into account man-made reclamation works as well as the natural build-up of shingle and sand deposits, more land has been gained from the sea along the east coast than has been yielded to it. But whether by erosion or accretion, this coast has for several hundred years been one on which it has been impossible to know without detailed reference to maps and records—and sometimes not even then—where "new land" began and "true land" ended, or where sea or land should be accorded ancient rights.

This, then, is the coastline that lay open to the exceptional conditions of 31st January 1953. It consisted of stretches of sand-dunes and shingle banks formed naturally by the sea and in some cases held together either by the planting of grasses and shrubs or by the placing of groynes; lengths of man-made defences, usually in the form of clay banks but including some concrete sea-walls or concrete reinforcements or revetments added to the clay; and occasional outcrops of soft cliff. By far the most extensive form of defence was (and still is) the clay bank. There were some 1,200 miles of these, many facing directly on to the beaches but many others the relics of earlier lines of defence which had been superseded by the build-up of beaches and marshland. Where these inner banks had been maintained they formed a valuable second line of defence, but in some places they had been deliberately removed and ploughed down, or breached to make roadways. Almost certainly, too, there had in some places been damage during the war due partly to neglect and partly to military activities along the shoreline.

The breach in the bank at Overy Staithe. It was this breach that caused the worst damage at Holkham and at the western end of Wells, trapping low-lying areas in a pincer movement.
Gilbert White

In some areas, natural and artificial barriers formed a double defence. Perhaps one of the most complex defence systems along the coast was on the Holkham estate in north Norfolk, owned by Lord Leicester. The Leicesters, descendants of the eighteenth century pioneer "scientific farmer" Coke of Norfolk, had devoted generations of effort to reclaiming the marshland between Scolt Head and Wells, turning what was originally saltings into good grazing land. The true coastline here consists of a range of sandhills and dunes, which have been stabilised by the planting of grasses and, on the central section opposite Holkham Hall itself, by plantations of pine established in the 1850s to protect the fields from blown sand. In addition, between half a mile and a mile behind the dunes is a complex of earthen banks of varying ages, enclosing the grazing land. To the west, at Deepdale Marsh and Norton Marsh, these banks are lapped by spring tides on the seaward side, but they nevertheless mark a gain of about half a mile over the seventeenth-century high-water mark, which reached the farms and cottages of the hamlet of

Burnham Norton; and indeed the high water of 31st January 1953 reached just this point. During that night, part of the sand-dunes to both east and west gave way, but the bank enclosing Deepdale and Norton Marshes held, the flooding behind it being caused by green seas pouring over the top. To the east, near Wells Harbour, the banks themselves gave way under pressure of the pincer movement of the sea from both the Overy and Wells inlets. The 1953 experience in this area, incidentally, illustrated how, once overcome by the sea, internal complexes of banks can prove a mixed blessing. Since they are built for defence from without, they tend to contain few sluices for draining off water from within — and these sluices need to be kept in constant repair. One observer of the aftermath of the 1953 disaster noted that "between Hunstanton and Wells, a great deal of the water on reclaimed land was still there in late February, and it had thus almost returned to the condition of the old coastline with lagoons and a long offshore bar". It was this standing water, rather than the flood itself, that did so much long-lasting harm to the soil in this area.

The inland waters of East Anglia also play their part in maintaining the balance between dry land and flood. The most obvious example is the Great Ouse, which flows northwards into the Wash, and the network of man-made cuts attendant upon it, all of them steeply banked as they flow across a fenland

Overy Staithe Bank after the flood. Breaches in the banks have caused a strange reversal of the norm. To the right of the bank, pasture-land is several feet under water, while on the left the marshes are relatively dry. *Gilbert White*

largely below sea level. As we shall see, the surge of the tide on the night of 31st January 1953 produced a tidal bore effect which in some places breached the river banks and in others overtopped them. Further round the coast, the Broads and other lakes behind the Norfolk and Suffolk coastlines were also to have an effect on the night's experiences, some of them overspilling and attacking from the rear towns and villages whose defences had withstood the direct onslaught of the sea. And it was fortunate, as the official report on the floods pointed out, that the inland waters had not been unduly swollen by rain or snow, as they might well have been at that time of year; had they been, the destruction in areas close to the rivers and lakes would have been indescribably worse.

One further aspect affecting the south-eastern quadrant of Britain needs to be mentioned before we turn to the meteorological events which led up to the disaster. This is the fact that the whole south-eastern coastline of Britain is gradually sinking — by nearly one foot per century — as the platform on which the British Isles stand tilts slowly on a north-east/south-west axis. The steady descent of the land is confirmed not only by tidal records, which show the increasing frequency of floods in coastal areas formerly tide-free, but also by archaeology. The Thames, for example, was apparently tidal in Roman times only about as far as London Bridge, whereas it is now tidal as far as Teddington, some thirteen miles upstream. In Essex, excavations have revealed several layers of remains of human settlements well below the present tideline; among them, domestic Romano-British remains at Canvey and Tilbury up to thirteen feet below high-water mark, and sherds from the Beaker culture ten feet deep under tidal silt. The evidence of a corresponding rise in the level of the land on the north-west coast of Great Britain confirms that what is taking place is indeed a settlement of the land mass towards the south-east rather than, as used to be thought, merely a rise in sea-level due to the melting of Polar ice — though this remains a secondary cause of the increasing encroachment of the sea.

On both sides of the North Sea, inhabitants of the lowlands have learned to live with the threat of the sea. It has been with them long enough to become a fact of life. Conditions similar to those of 1953 (though, perhaps surprisingly, not identified closely until 1928) have been responsible for a series of disasters, the greatest on record having been the "St Elizabeth's Flood" of 18th November 1421, which swept away seventy-two Dutch villages with the loss of over 10,000 lives. There was another great flood in 1607, when the sea broke in between Great Yarmouth and Happisburgh in Norfolk, devastating the farmland behind. It was as a result of this flood that, two years later, Sea Breach Commissioners were appointed by Parliament to restore the defences and keep them in order, a responsibility which they carried out until 1930, though apparently with variable diligence. No doubt the Sea Breach Com-

Enfield Highway
Library
Hertford Road
Enfield 443-2300

missioners suffered from the same problems as Turnpike Trustees, in that they were largely dependent upon the community spirit of the locals.

In more recent times, and in England at least, the more serious floods along the east coast seem to have followed a cycle of twenty-five to thirty years. Northerly gales coinciding with a spring tide on 29th November 1897 caused breaches in the sea defences in Norfolk and Suffolk and severe flooding along almost the entire coastline from Harwich to Southend, as well as at a number of places along the north bank of the Thames Estuary. Fortunately, the peak of the tide fell in the middle of the day, and for this reason there was no loss of life. However, a resident of Horsey in north-east Norfolk, where the sea broke through, had some caustic comments on the work of the Sea Breach Commissioners. "Keeping out the sea," he wrote, "is not a one man and a boy job as some of the Commissioners fare to think it is. Why, there was one Commissioner, he says to me, 'What's wanting is plenty of faggots.' Says I to him, 'Sir, there were faggots enough all ready to be used long before the storm came, but no one was told to use them.' 'Ah,' he says, 'that was very wrong. It ought to teach us a lesson.' Say I, 'Some folks take a deal of teaching,' and he laughed. But, think I, it isn't a laughing matter." Faggots—bundles of sticks tied together which swelled and held the water when in position—were the staple of sea defences before sandbags took their place. They were, indeed, a staple of civil engineering in the nineteenth century, not only protecting Britain's coastal land from encroachment but also enabling railway-builders to carry their tracks across such wastes as Chat Moss and Rannoch Moor. But they are not suitable as emergency equipment; they are prime building material, not for use as stop-gaps. So the Horsey critic's barbs were misdirected; the faggots should have been used to build up a permanent sea-wall, not kept to one side for use when the spring tide threatened.

Then, in January 1928, a night-time flood ravaged the east coast and finally drove up the Thames, drowning fourteen basement-dwellers in central London. It was this calamity that led eventually to the giant Thames flood prevention scheme which in 1977, after nearly fifty years and logarithmic multiplications of costs, was at last under construction. The 1928 flood also led to the first scientific analysis of the phenomenon of the surge, of which more later.

So the historical evidence suggests that severe flooding, though not necessarily on the scale of 1953, is inevitable along the east coast from time to time, and that the conditions producing the greatest risk can be defined with some accuracy, though prediction is not so easy. The worst floods have been caused by the combination of spring tides with high winds from the north, with the precise direction of the winds, their duration, and their coincidence with the tides being the critical factors. In 1897, a depression moving across southern England from the south-west, which would normally have had a dampening effect on the spring tide, suddenly veered at the critical time before high-water so that north-by-north-west winds whipped the seas towards the Essex coast. In 1928 there was a similar movement of the wind, and on this occasion the flood damage in riverside areas was increased because of recent heavy snow and rainfall which had swelled the inland waters. In 1953 there was, as we shall see, the common factor of a "surge" in the North Sea, but meteorological conditions were rather different. "The usual tidal oscillation of sea-level around our coasts," one researcher has noted, "is predictable for many years in advance with a very high degree of accuracy, but is subject to sudden and often large errors in the prediction due to the prevailing meteorological conditions." It is the combination of the two factors, tide and weather, together with such captious elements as timing, the duration of the wind, its possible veering, to say nothing of general meteorological and hydrographic conditions well beyond the site of potentially disastrous floods, that limits the potential for effective forecasting or preventive measures. Not until after the 1953 floods were tide and weather brought together within the

Coastguard Scott of Lowestoft watches the surge at its height from the lookout on the North Sea Wall. After this photograph was taken, he was to be cut off for nearly three hours.

Ford Jenkins

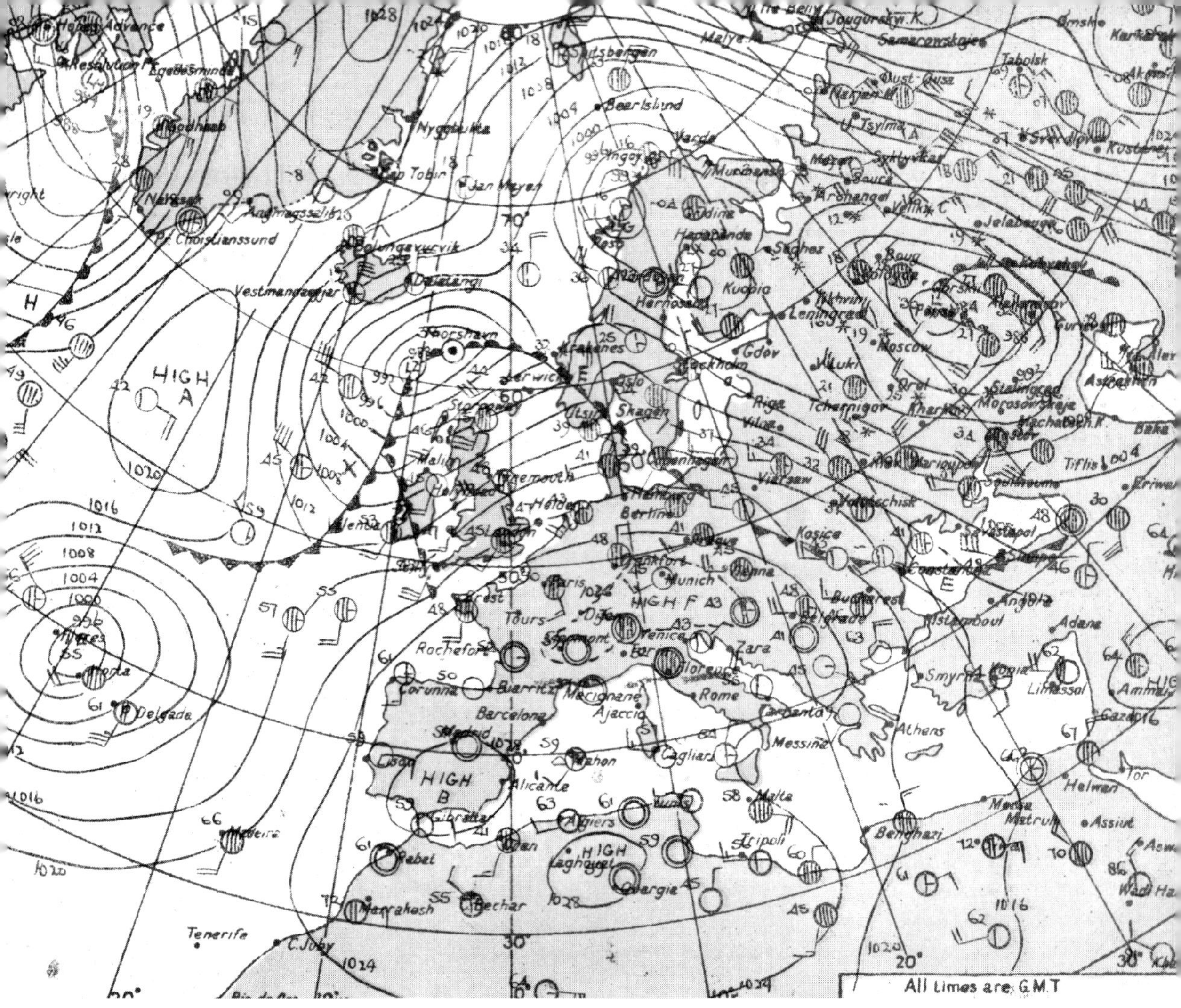

Weather in the North Atlantic at midday on Friday, 30th January 1953. The depression Low Z appears near 60°N, between Iceland and north-west Scotland.

Crown Copyright reserved. Reproduced with the permission of the Controller of Her Majesty's Stationery Office

purview of a common storm warning service, but even today, with all the modern technical resources at its disposal, this service has by no means solved all the forecasting problems; and even when storm warnings, based on precise and accurate data, have been issued those responsible for translating these into action are called upon to make nice judgements between the local risk of flooding on the one hand and the danger of crying wolf on the other. These problems are examined in greater detail in a later chapter, but it is necessary to mention them here in setting the scene for the 1953 disaster because there was, after the flood, a good deal of wisdom after the event, not all of it unjustified.

According to some estimates, the water-level registered in 1953 is not likely to recur for another two hundred years, though if the sinking of the land mass already referred to continues at the present rate this expectation-span will be reduced to one hundred years by the year 2053. But these are statistical projections, and the comfort they might give must be set against the comparatively short period of observation on which they are based—about eighty years—and the fact that another set of figures from the same source shows that the frequency of abnormally high tides on the east coast has increased progressively by four times since 1820.

In the pre-satellite 1950s, the primary source for weather forecasting was regular observation from hundreds of reporting stations—lighthouses, coastguards, airfields, ocean weather ships, ordinary shipping going about its business, and even enthusiastic amateurs. In Britain, all this information was collated at the Meteorological Office headquarters, then at Dunstable in Bedfordshire, and used to produce weather charts at six-hourly intervals similar in appearance to the "Atlantic charts" shown in B.B.C. Television's weather forecasts.

As far as Britain, and for that matter the whole of north-western Europe, is concerned, the Atlantic is the most significant area in weather forecasting. Conditions across the ocean are monitored by an international force of ocean weather ships permanently on station at predetermined positions, and their reports are amplified by those from merchant and Royal Navy ships on the Meteorological Office's reporting list. It was from a merchantman to the south-west of Iceland that forecasters at Dunstable first heard of the developing depression that was to wreak such havoc over the British Isles and the sea-board of north-west Europe as January 1953 passed into February.

The merchant ship's routine report at mid-day on Thursday 29th January mentioned a developing disturbance in the area, identified at the Meteorological Office as a depression that had broken away from the existing low pressure area north of the Azores. At the time, it did not seem particularly significant; it was merely part of the complex pressure system that builds up over the North Atlantic in late winter, producing extremely stormy conditions in Britain towards the end of January and the beginning of February six years out of every seven. The main feature of the Atlantic weather picture that Thursday remained the almost stationary depression just north of the Azores, with the newcomer, christened "Low Z", a comparatively minor blemish on the classic late January weather pattern.

Through the night of Thursday to Friday, Low Z continued to move slowly north-eastwards, deepening as it went. By 6 a.m. on Friday it had become the dominant feature of the Atlantic map, the earlier depression having faded away. Low Z was by now close to the Ocean Weather Ship *Weather Explorer's* position at 58°53′N 18°48′W, and its pressure had sunk menacingly low to

988 millibars, eight below the norm. At 1.30 p.m. *Weather Explorer* reported that Low Z was bringing a degree of disturbance in its wake. A squall was observed approaching the ship from the north-west; pressure suddenly fell, and there were "turbulent precipitous waves and driving spray". Later in the afternoon, Low Z accelerated and turned slightly eastwards towards the Hebrides. At Dunstable, the routine response of a normal gale warning was all that at this stage seemed necessary.

The first north-westerly winds, veering northerly as Low Z gathered speed and moved on towards Norway, were now being felt in Scotland. By any reckoning, leaving aside the question of tides and the possibility of a "surge", this was going to be a gale to remember. During the night of Friday to Saturday the depression, deepening now to below 970 millibars, made a sudden south-eastward lunge down over the North Sea. Large tracts of the great Scottish forests were laid waste, the number of trees felled by the wind during those few hours equalling the normal cull of a whole year. Over on the east coast of Scotland, at R.A.F. Kinloss, the cups of the anemometer sped round to record a wind-speed of 113 m.p.h., noted by the Air Ministry as "one of the highest gusts ever recorded in Britain"—though it was beaten at Costa Hill, in the Orkneys, where there was one gust of 125 m.p.h. during a period in which the *average* wind-speed was 90 m.p.h.

The great gale was already claiming its first victims. Somewhere off Barra Head in the Hebrides, the fifteen-man crew of the Fleetwood trawler *Michael Griffith* vanished in the boiling seas; this was the first of ten ships to sink before the gale had blown itself out.

At about 7.45 on Saturday morning, the six-year-old British Railways car ferry *Princess Victoria*, with a crew of forty-nine and 125 passengers aboard, cast off at Stranraer and began to struggle up Loch Ryan to the Irish Sea on her regular crossing to Larne. A warning of severe gales had been in force for the area for some five hours, and the wind was already blowing N.N.W. force eight to nine, with gusts to force eleven. Rounding Milleur Point at the head of the loch, the *Princess Victoria* suddenly met the full force of the gale. Her stern car-loading doors were burst open and buckled, and at once she began to take in water on the car deck. Her cargo shifted and she began to list to starboard. At 9.46 a.m. she radioed for the help of a tug, but she wallowed for a further 45 minutes before the first S.O.S. was sent. It was about two in the afternoon when, still unlocated by the aircraft and ships sent to search for her, and with her wireless operator still transmitting, she keeled over and sank, having drifted, ironically, across the Irish Sea to a point close to the comparative calm of Belfast Lough. The death-toll was 132 and included all the women and children on board, who had been thrown into the sea when their lifeboat was overturned as it was being launched.

The situation at 06.00 hours on Saturday, 31st January 1953. Low Z is now moving round Scotland, and has deepened further. The forecast, issued at noon on Saturday, was that "all districts will have gale force winds, severe in many places, and squally showers, mainly of hail or snow". ⇨

Crown Copyright reserved. Reproduced with the permission of the Controller of Her Majesty's Stationery Office

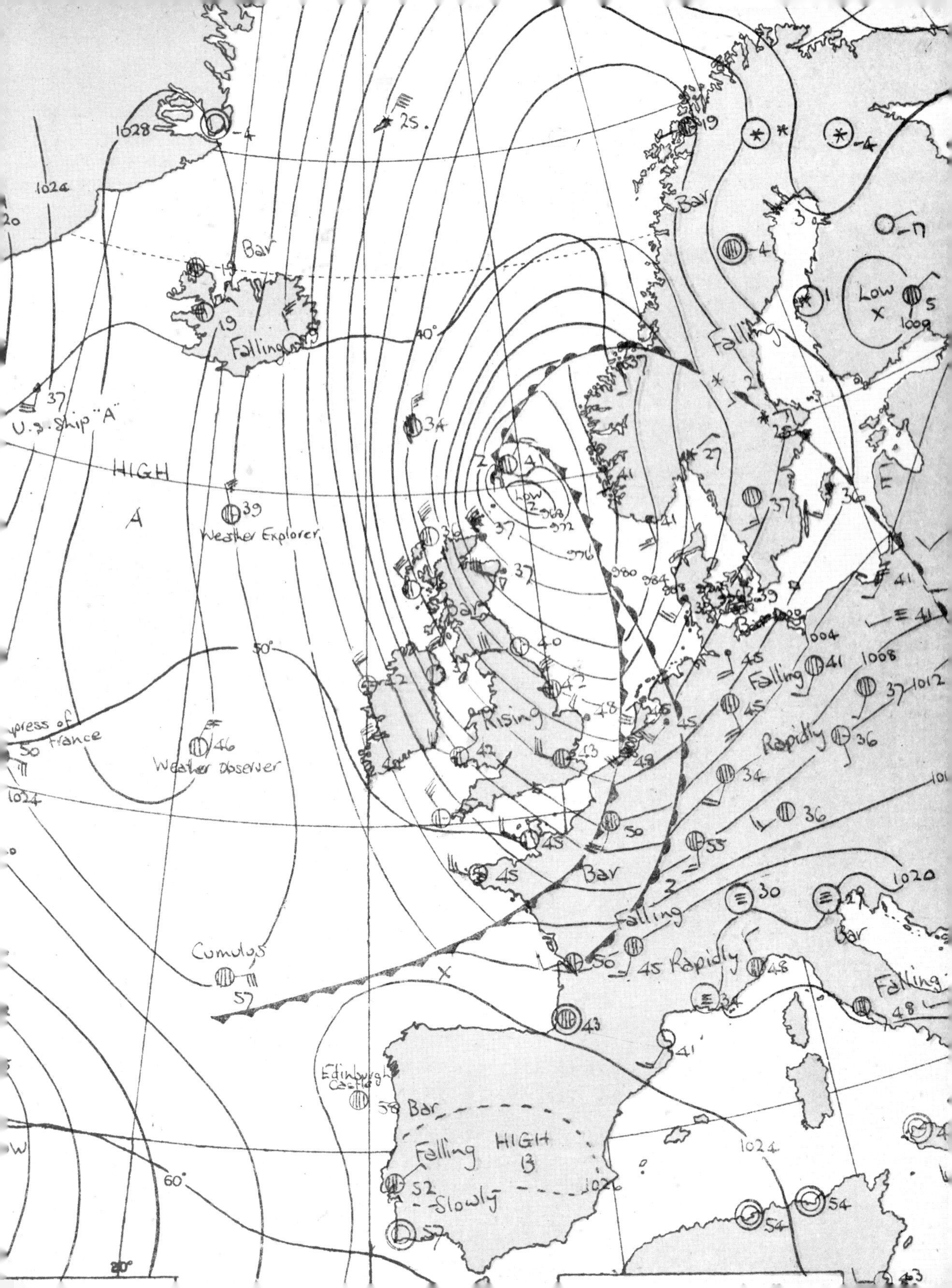

1028
1024
Bar
Falling
U.S. Ship "A"
HIGH
A
Weather Explorer
40°
Low
Low
Falling
Bar
Rising
Falling
Rapidly
50°
Empress of France
Weather Observer
1024
Bar
Falling
45 Rapidly
1020
Bar
Falling
Cumulus
Edinburgh Castle
Bar
Falling
HIGH
B
Slowly
60°
1024
1004
1008
1012

The particular horror of the loss of the *Princess Victoria*, which was to become the lead story in the B.B.C.'s radio news bulletins for the remainder of the day—television news did not yet exist in any real sense—was that disaster had overtaken a routine ferry crossing such as thousands of people took regularly, whether across the Irish Sea, the North Sea or the English Channel. British Railways cross-channel steamers have the familiarity and sturdy dependability of a London Transport bus, and so the sinking of the *Princess Victoria* came to be seen as a disaster for everyman. Ironically, the attention paid to it by radio and newspaper sub-editors on this basis to some extent obscured the greater disaster which was striking Britain at the very moment that the words were being heard or read. The tragedy of the ship seemed very close, I remember, at Newhaven, where I heard about it on the nine o'clock news that night. Newhaven is essentially a one-industry town, and that industry is the cross-channel service. It was as if the ship's captain who lived across the road and the seaman who lived next door had escaped death only by a hairsbreadth. There were similar reflections, according to an account written at the time, among the guests at a Saturday night dance in the railwaymen's club at Harwich, where the announcement of the disaster was followed by a few minutes of stunned silence. Harwich's own trials were then, as it turned out, less than an hour away.

Meanwhile, as the *Princess Victoria* wallowed off Milleur Point, the gale swept southwards. At Southampton, it was decided to postpone the sailing of the *Queen Mary*, due to leave that morning. At 11.30 a.m., the Meteorological Office warned river and catchment boards in East Anglia that "exceptionally strong north-west to north winds are becoming established over the North Sea". This was to seem, in the light of subsequent events, a rather tame message. The official report on the floods concentrated on preventive measures for future occasions rather than on laying blame for the 1953 disaster, but popular feeling in the afflicted areas was—and is still—that stronger words might have been used, and might have received wider circulation. But this, like each of its kind, was a novel situation, and it was being faced, in the case of the river and catchment boards, less than a year after reorganisation. Official complacency is a tempting and obvious target in any post mortem on a disaster. There is certainly some criticism to be made of the failure of national government to react to the situation once it had come about, as will be seen later, but there was no suggestion in the official report that any more effective warnings, under the system operating at the time, could have been given. Much has changed since 1953, of course, in the pattern of public information, and given a similar situation today fewer people, even outside the hours of broadcasting, would be caught unawares.

Holland, however, has far longer been conscious of the potential threat of the sea, for obvious reasons. It has had a flood warning system in operation

By 06.00 on Sunday, 1st February, Low Z has moved away across northern Germany and is filling. "The strong to gale force northerly winds still affecting eastern districts will steadily moderate", said the forecast. But by this time, Low Z's work was done, bringing havoc to eastern England, Belgium and Holland.

Crown Copyright reserved. Reproduced with the permission of the Controller of Her Majesty's Stationery Office

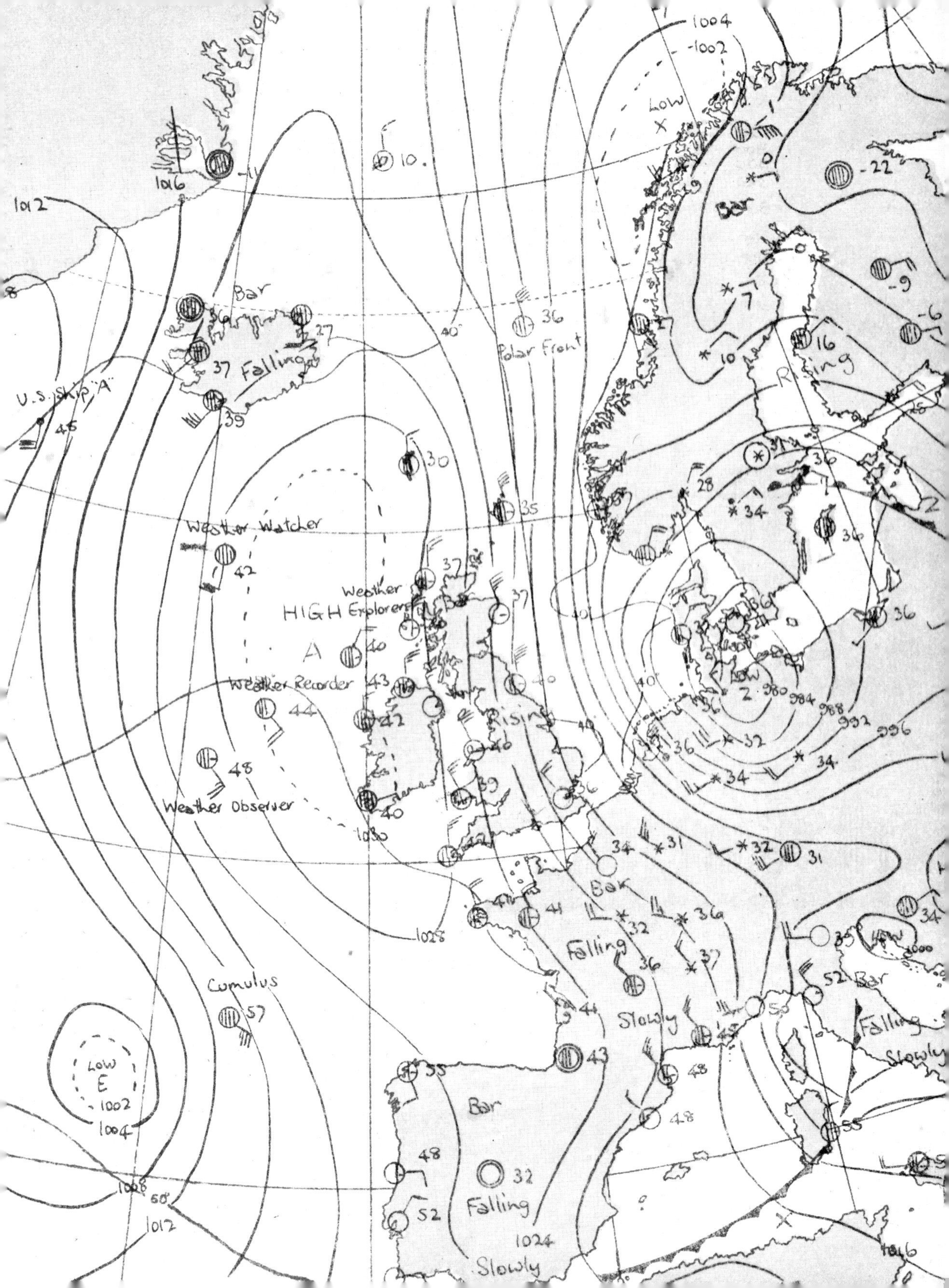

1004
1002
Low
X
1016
1012
10.
-22
Bar
Bar
27
36
Polar Front
40°
37 Falling
U.S. Ship 'A'
45
39
-9
-6
16
10
Rising
30
28
34
36
35
Weather Watcher
42
37
Weather
HIGH Explorer
37
A
40
Weather Recorder
43
44
40
Rising
Low
Z
980
984
988
992
996
36
32
34
34
48
Weather Observer
40
1030
39
34
31
32
31
Bar
41
41
32
36
Falling
36
37
1028
Low
1000
35
52
Bar
Cumulus
57
Slowly
43
55
Falling
Slowly
48
Low
E
1002
1004
Bar
48
55
48
32
1008
60°
52
Falling
1012
1024
Slowly
1016

since 1916, involving the sending of telegrams to local and government authorities and, later, broadcasts to the public in weather and news bulletins. The Dutch system put out a warning at 10 a.m. on Saturday 31st January of "rather high tides", subsequently strengthened at 4.45 p.m. to one of "dangerously high tides". References to the tide were absent from the British Meteorological Office's warnings, for very good administrative reasons that will become apparent later and which were subsequently taken care of; the noon forecast, for example, spoke only of "northerly gales of exceptional severity" — a cue, perhaps, to put up the storm shutters, if one had them, but no adequate preparation for the likelihood of the sea breaking down the front door.

Nonetheless, the widespread feeling remains that "they", whoever they might be, were caught on the hop. A large proportion of the people I have spoken or written to while writing this book touch upon this in one way or another, and certainly most of the accounts of the night of the flood show that the water burst upon most of its victims unexpectedly. While hundreds of people in East Anglia were fleeing to the top floors of their homes, or even climbing out on to the roofs, the B.B.C.'s bulletins still spoke only in the most general terms of gales and heavy seas. Some critics of the prevailing official blandness that night subsequently placed the blame with the Postmaster-General, who had failed in 1950 to secure a radio wavelength for the continuation of Airmet, a continuous weather report and forecast service which had been operated by the Meteorological Office on long-wave since just before the Second World War. In fact, it is unlikely that many of Airmet's audience, consisting mainly of amateur sailors and airmen with a sprinkling of idle knob-twiddlers trying to find Radio Luxembourg, would have been listening as the dark gathered on a winter's evening. When the Waverley Committee came, after the event, to consider the question of public warnings, it rejected on Home Office advice the use of the B.B.C. on the grounds that unnecessary alarm might be caused in areas not immediately threatened, preferring to rely on the police in specific areas. It may be noted here that even in 1953, when local policemen were rather thicker on the ground than they are today, this recommendation was not too impressive when applied to areas like north Norfolk, where scattered communities were often well beyond the reach, within a limited time, of a single local bobby. In fact, the development of regional television and local radio has altered the strategy recommended in the Waverley Report, and broadcast warnings are now regarded as a vital element in the warning system.

But the basic defect in 1953 was, as the Waverley Report pointed out, that responsibility for reporting and forecasting conditions likely to lead to severe flooding was divided between the Meteorological Office, which looked after the wind, as it were, and the Admiralty's Hydrographic Department, which dealt with the moods of the sea. The latter was, in any case, essentially a long-range forecasting department which regarded its work as over once its tide tables for the ensuing year had been published; and even if it had access to day-to-day information it had no means of disseminating that information in a hurry. The Waverley Report proposed, and the recommendation was later adopted, that the two services should get together during the critical period of the year, from mid-September to the end of April, and operate a joint warning system from the Meteorological Office. This system is described in more detail in a later chapter.

But all this was in the wisdom of hindsight. It takes two to make a quarrel, and it takes a combination of at least two factors to make a disaster. In the case of the 1953 floods, two factors were indeed involved: one was the tide, a predictable quantity; the second was more capricious, the "X" factor of the North Sea surge.

High tide on the night of Saturday to Sunday 31st January to 1st February 1953 was a full moon spring tide, though it was not as high, discounting the effect of the surge, as either of the new moon spring tides before and after it. If it had been, as the Waverley Report noted, "given the same distribution and sequence of winds and atmospheric pressure, the disaster would have been worse". The tide was due at Immingham Dock at 6.55 p.m., at Kings Lynn at 7.35, at Great Yarmouth at 10.00, at Canvey Island at 01.47 a.m., and at London Bridge at 03.07. As it turned out, factor "X", the surge, was the more dominant influence on the behaviour of the sea that night, and none of these timings was exactly kept. The time-lag between surge and high tide, which was not constant, is one of the difficulties met with in trying to piece together the story of the night's events, especially as actual flooding was the result in some places of a sudden breakthrough of sea-water and in others of later breaches or seepages. And the few eye-witnesses who were about in the early stages were more concerned with immediate impressions than with accurate timekeeping. As a Ministry of Agriculture report noted, "farmers had little or no warning other than from those few who were outside during the evening and noticed that inland drains suddenly began to flow upstream". In Holland, first impressions were even more terrifying: "From reports by several eye-witnesses it appears that the last and most disastrous surge of the sea before the high tide of Sunday morning occurred very suddenly and had the character of a tidal bore."

The phenomenon of the North Sea surge, although it has been satisfactorily defined only since the 1928 flood, is easy to understand—so easy, indeed, that one wonders why no one had thought of it before. High winds blowing on the surface of the sea build up a wall of water, assisted by changes in atmospheric pressures which tend to drag water out of high-pressure into low-pressure areas. As the Waverley Report said: "A surge which has been

This aerial view of flood damage near Spurn Head, Yorkshire was one of the dramatic pictures brought back by the R.A.F.'s survey teams, operating from Benson, Oxfordshire. It was pictures like this that first revealed to ground-based officials just how extensive and calamitous the floods had been. *Press Association*

produced in the northern part of the North Sea travels into the southern part of the sea and up estuaries in the same way as the tide. The crests of both tide and surge take about twelve hours to travel from the north-east of Scotland to the mouth of the Thames. Because of the rotation of the earth, the water is deflected to the right of the tidal currents . . . and hence, while the crests are travelling southwards the water levels of both tide and surge are higher on the east coast of England than elsewhere. Tide and surge are partially deflected from the southern end of the North Sea and in the northward movement the highest levels are on the coast of Holland." On the night of 31st January 1953, the surge reached, and may even in places have exceeded, ten feet—this in addition, of course, to the predicted height of the spring tide.

The surge ran ahead of the tide, according to most accounts by about an hour and a half. The effect was of an exceptionally high tide which, since it preceded the true tide and persisted longer, was unduly protracted and would, even without the physical battering of storm-driven waves, have severely tested the sea-defences. At 3 p.m. on the Saturday, according to one account, "gale-force north winds were affecting all the western half of the North Sea, but in the southern part the winds remained north-west, maintaining an east-west water gradient". Three hours later, "the southward movement of water was being accelerated and the level in the Thames Estuary had started to rise". By 9 p.m., the surge had reached its peak, with a rise of eight feet stretching between Norfolk and Holland.

Such analyses have, of course, the benefit of having been written later with access to records. The impression of observers on the ground was of the sweep of the surge down the east coast of Britain and a succession of incidents which were regarded at the time as merely of local significance. In mid-afternoon, with high tide still an hour away, the Tees overflowed its banks. By teatime, the surge was tearing at the sea-walls of Lincolnshire. It sped on, slamming into the dead-end of the Wash with tremendous force, only a little of which was expended in driving up the open mouth of the Great Ouse, and overspilling round the coast of East Anglia and into the Thames Estuary, and then, deflected northwards, completing its night of destruction by hitting Holland and Belgium, taking some 2,000 lives with it. Whipped up by the wind, driven along ahead of the spring tide, dragged southwards by the force of Low Z—by now a depression recovering from its atmospheric nadir—the North Sea emptied itself in the north to spill disastrously over the lowlands to the south. The cruel twist of fate was in the timing; by the time the surge reached Felixstowe, Jaywick and Canvey Island, people were in bed and, as they had put their lights out, had become almost inevitable victims.

We shall never have an overall picture of what happened that night. It was not a time for eye-witnesses to be about, and once the sea had struck it was a matter of survival and rescue rather than conjecture on what the sea had done or how it had done it. But there is some evidence to suggest that the surge was not quite the bolt from the blue that official accounts suggest. For example, there is the account of Kings Lynn ambulance driver Bertie Hart—someone, as he describes himself, "who has lived by and watched the river Great Ouse for sixty years and gets used to its moods and changes". For three days, Mr Hart had noticed that "outgoing tides were not getting away as they should have done. There was a lot of water still in the river when the incoming tides came". Kings Lynn, facing north into the Wash, was of course directly in line for the first intimation of the great surge that was coming, and it may be that Mr Hart, with his sensitivity to the ways of the Wash, was one of the first people in England to feel uneasy as January 1953 drew to a close.

But he was not alone. On the Saturday afternoon, he went to a local football match and got into conversation there with one of the river pilots who had been at sea the night before. "He told me," Mr Hart says, "that the motion of the sea had been strange, like something he had never experienced before."

"We were very much concerned about the wind," Mr Hart goes on, "but never did we think about floods."

I have come across no one else who claims to have noticed tidal peculiarities earlier than the Saturday of the flood, but there is some backing for the view that the early tide on that day was already being visibly influenced by the impending surge. "Observers say that the evening tide was early owing to the holding-up of the ebb," reported one scientific commentator, while an Essex policeman, looking out casually over the Blackwater estuary, noticed that the afternoon tide appeared not to go back at all — "the wind seemed to be holding the water". All this would seem to suggest, if no more, that while surges are not predictable in advance their first intimations are observable even by relative amateurs, and that these observations should somehow be fed into the defence system. Curiously, the Waverley Report does not appear to have considered this aspect of hydrographic forecasting, despite the fact that such field observations, including those of amateurs, have been a staple of the meteorological service for many years.

As we shall see, there is no accounting for the timing of what happened on the night of 31st January 1953. A housewife in Wells-next-the-Sea, on the north Norfolk coast, was already putting up flood shutters before residents in Mablethorpe, Lincolnshire, who were shortly to be drowned, were aware of anything more than a wild night. It is no journalistic fancy to suggest that on that night the North Sea went mad. The north Norfolk coast seems to have caught the full force of wind and surge and tide before areas to the north which, according to Admiralty tables and Meteorological Office orthodoxy, should have been hit first. Even adjacent villages were stricken hours apart, according to whether the water that reached them came from breached banks (as in a comparatively small number of cases) or from green seas breaking over the bank-tops, as was more common, or from the sudden yielding of the banks of inland waters, as happened at Great Yarmouth.

Some defences gave way fairly early on in the assault; others yielded only after prolonged attack. "The flooding was not caused so much by breaches in the dykes," said one account, "as by the actual submersion of their tops. The breaches that did occur resulted mainly from the fall of water on the clay fill on the inner dyke faces when it came over the top, as well as from its tremendous pressure, which also broke inner dykes not normally exposed to sea action." Thus in some places the sea came in some time after the danger seemed to have passed.

By the afternoon of Saturday 31st January, the sea was hammering mercilessly at the eastern coastline. It smashed huge gaps in Scarborough's massive North Bay sea-wall. Sweeping down past Spurn Head and curling inwards, the storm cut off the community of lifeboatmen and coastguards on the headland and carried away the transmission masts of the Humber radio station. Racing on to Cleethorpes, it smashed the railway embankment and swept away buildings on the foreshore. Large areas of neighbouring Grimsby were flooded. But this was, as yet, merely severe storm damage—bad enough, but within the scope of the emergency services. The worst was yet to come.

Damage to the sea-wall at Mablethorpe. *Press Association*

CHAPTER TWO

"THE SEA attacked in two ways," said one report. "Waves dashed against the sea-walls and sand-dunes . . . until they were tattered and breached. (Then) the sea, coming up the estuaries, over-topped and breached river banks, in many places inundating coastal towns from the rear. 'Stabs in the back' seems an apt description of most of the incidents, and clearly the main lesson of the flood is that the back of any sea defence work needs to be considered just as carefully as the front."

One of the difficulties faced by subsequent enquiries was that, in the words of the same report, "there are no eye-witnesses to describe precisely how each wall failed". By the time the surge swept into the Wash and began to pound the vulnerable coast of East Anglia, darkness had fallen. Sunset was at 4.47 p.m. It had been blowing hard all day, and many people living round the coast had spent the afternoon securing their boats, shoring up shrubs and trees, and generally battening everything down in readiness for a wild night, though just how wild they were not yet to know. It was a night for staying indoors, drawing closer to the fire, and listening to "Saturday Night Theatre" on the radio, for television reception in East Anglia in 1953 was still sketchy and erratic. At Marsh House Farm, near Burnham Overy on the north Norfolk coast, farmer Peter Hancock returned from a windswept afternoon's pigeon-shooting—"there was so much wind, the pigeons couldn't rise", he remembers—and tried to get warm over treacle and toast in front of the fire. Bertie Hart of Kings Lynn says: "I don't believe anyone really saw the actual flooding, owing to the incoming tide and the darkness."

It was about five o'clock that afternoon that a neighbour knocked at the door of Mrs Madeleine Swinn in Wells-next-the-Sea. There was a high tide already washing the quay, she said; would Mrs Swinn help her cover her grating to the cellar with sandbags to keep the water out? There were still more than two hours to go before high water, but Wells is directly in line for the first intimations of a surge moving southwards down the North Sea.

"We collected clinker from a neighbour who lived on higher ground," Mrs Swinn recalls, "and found on our return that we were up to our ankles in water."

When Mrs Swinn got back to her own house in Freeman Street, water was seeping through her front door. "Like an idiot," she remembers, "I got a large bowl and began mopping up"—an echo of the story of the legendary Mrs Partington of Sidmouth, whose attempts to sweep the sea away with a broom

A 160-ton motor torpedo boat carried out of Wells Harbour by the surge and deposited on the quay. It became one of the local wonders of the flood, and when, several months later, it was hoisted back into the water, scores of people from the town and villages around turned out to watch. *Walmsley and Webb*

were much quoted in Victorian politics as a simile for reactionary policy. But, seeing the futility of mopping up against the encroaching sea, Mrs Swinn turned to barricading her door with cushions. Soon this became all too evidently a waste of time, and she prepared to retreat upstairs and wait for her husband to come home.

"Finally he came in through a front window, having been carried across the road, which by this time was a torrent. We both tried getting rid of the rising water until there was a terrific noise, and our outside buildings were knocked down. We just had time to get up the stairway, up to our knees in water. After that we felt safe, but we only had an oil lamp as the electricity had broken down. We heard later that Overy Staithe Bank had given way and so we were between the two rushing waters and the whole of the marshes were covered."

At Marsh House Farm, Peter Hancock noticed that the pond in front of his farmhouse seemed to be overflowing. The 'phone rang, and his wife Mary answered. It was someone calling to say that the sea had broken through at Overy Staithe and to ask if the Hancocks were all right. "But the bank's a mile away," said Mrs Hancock. "The sea can't come this far." But her husband opened the front door on his way out to check that the cattle were bedded down for the night, and there was the sea, lapping the step. "My God, it *is* the sea!" he yelled. With a three-year-old son upstairs and his wife "vastly pregnant", as she says, with a second, Peter Hancock's first instinct was to get out. Within minutes they were running to the car. After finding the coast road already impassable, they eventually traced a route across higher ground to the safety of Mr Hancock's parents' house in the next village.

The Hancocks' farmer neighbour, Harris Wroth, decided to brave the wind and drive the two miles or so to his local, the Victoria at Holkham. ("You must want a drink pretty badly to go out on a night like this," said his wife.) He had just ordered his first drink when someone came in and said that there was water up to the steps outside. "Don't be silly," said Mr Wroth, "I've just this minute come in." But it was true, and he was soon to find himself ferrying a car-load of refugees to safety along the inside bank of Holkham Park.

One motorist on the Holkham road met the wall of water coming towards him. Thinking at first that it was the kind of temporary flooding not uncommon on this road in winter, he drove on – until the car was floating. He scrambled out and found the wall surrounding Holkham Park. Sitting astride it, he heaved himself along by his arms until he reached a stranded bus whose passengers took him aboard, in a state of complete exhaustion.

The sea had come through at Meals, to the east, as well as at Overy Staithe. West of Overy Staithe Bank is the inlet of the River Burn and then another series of curving banks enclosing Norton Marsh, Deepdale Marsh and the hamlet of Burnham Norton. At about the same time as Mrs Swinn was trying to mop up at her front door in Wells, farm worker Betty Raven was setting out for her evening rounds of Marsh Farm at Burnham Norton. The lane from her own house slopes down to a sharp corner where, suddenly, the farm, Norton Marsh and Norton Bank beyond all come into view. As she rounded the corner, Betty Raven saw what she momentarily thought was snow on the bank. It wasn't snow; it was the foaming sea, poised to spill over on to the marshes.

Meanwhile, Wells butcher Charles Ramm had shut up shop for the night and was getting ready to leave when someone ran in from the street. "You'd better come at once," the visitor said. "There's a wall of water coming through on the marsh." On 600 acres between Wells and Holkham, Mr Ramm kept over seventy store cattle and more than 200 sheep.

"We couldn't get anywhere near," Mr Ramm remembers. "We could see some of the cattle had got up on to the manure heap. About all we could do that night was to get the dog out. We found him in the stable, standing in the crib with his front paws up on the wall to keep his nose out of the water. We got him out about eleven o'clock."

In the Lincolnshire coastal villages surrounding Mablethorpe and Sutton-on-Sea, the surge had already claimed its first victims, later to total forty. In Kings Lynn and along the west-facing shore of the Wash between Kings Lynn and Hunstanton, it was about to take over sixty more lives.

Between Lynn and Hunstanton, on an inland rise, is the village of Snettisham with, two miles away, its satellite settlement of Snettisham Beach. This was in 1953 a rather untidy piece of coastal development – the sort of thing most people thought that the Town and County Planning Acts would do away with – including an assortment of self-built bungalows, timber and asbestos shacks, beach-huts and chalets, caravans, a holiday camp, boats left there for the winter by weekend sailors from Kings Lynn and the towns of the East Midlands, and, by what must surely have been a planning blunder, a shingle extraction works. Some of the bungalows were holiday homes. Others were occupied by retired people, with a smattering of other residents glad to find any kind of roof over their heads in the acute housing shortage of the time. Away from the coast and on rising ground, Snettisham itself consisted of more substantial houses whose owners had perhaps been attracted by the proximity of the Sandringham estate and the existence of a rail link — now closed — with Lynn and London.

H. W. Temple Cole was living at that time at Newbridge House, some way from the sea. For him, the first hint of trouble came with a 'phone call from a friend in Kings Lynn at about 6.15 p.m. With high tide still eighty minutes away, she reported, there was sea-water in the streets of Lynn, and her husband had set out for Snettisham Beach with two other friends to check the safety of their boats and bungalows.

"As soon as we heard this," Mr Temple Cole said in an account written a few days later, "we both piled into the car and dashed off down to the beach, as we knew from the 1949 floods that if it was as high as they said, with a full day of gale-force north-west wind behind it, there was bound to be serious trouble." For Mr Temple Cole, it was the beginning of a full night of activity.

"We got as far as the first bend in the road where the holiday camp is, about half a mile from the beach front," he went on, "and were met by water across the road and a crowd of people who were already escaping from the tide. We at once realised the seriousness of the situation, as the water had not only come over the

It took some time to mobilise heavy earth-moving and road-building equipment to the task of restoring communications. The efforts of this tipper lorry seem quite inadequate — yet "first aid" to the life of East Anglia was dependant on local resources. *Walmsley and Webb*

actual beach but must also have breached the inner clay flood bank. We turned round at once, and picked up about five who were escaping, including an old man who had just come out of bed after being bedridden for some months, and dashed off with them up to the station pub, where they were taken in front of the fire. On the way we passed our friends from Kings Lynn on their way down, and slowed down to shout to them to pick up some more who were escaping."

Mr Temple Cole must have been one of the first of the many thousands round the coast who were to be engaged in rescue work that night. Meanwhile, there was already a full alert in Lynn. When Bertie Hart reported for duty at the police station at about 6.30 p.m., his arrival coincided with that of the borough surveyor and his foreman, who immediately swung into action. Mr Hart was sent to pick up an old ex-Army lorry, whose high wheel-base would clear at least some of the flood water, and given a roving commission to do what he could in the streets of the town. Trees were down, lorries had been abandoned in the water, and electricity sub-stations had short-circuited and were on fire.

"The flood water," recalls Mr Hart, "had got in a mile or so, and further in drains and dykes, right through the centre of Kings Lynn on the east side, and the river bank had broken on the west side. There were several railway embankments where the water was trapped and could not get away when the tide began to turn. On the Saddlebow Road there were three cars upside down, and forty-gallon drums of oil had been rolled along by the force of the water, knocking down the side of a house before falling into the River Nar."

But it was the stretch of coast between Hunstanton and Kings Lynn that took the brunt of the sea's assault upon Norfolk. "The most terrible scene of the disaster," wrote the county planning officer later, "was south of Hunstanton, where the natural bank, though strengthened, was overwhelmed. The majority of the dwellings built on it, including some permanently occupied, were destroyed or damaged and sixty-one people lost their lives."

At their bungalow on Snettisham beach, the Beckerton family had had a lively afternoon. Frederick and Vera Beckerton had recently bought their first television set, and had invited two of their children's friends in to see the Saturday tea-time programme. Earlier in the day, there had been a great deal of baking, and it was a flushed and excited party that settled down round the set after tea: Mr and Mrs Beckerton, their adopted daughter Hazel, who was twelve, and sons Michael, nine, and John, seven, together with two London foster-children, eleven-year-old Shirley Baxter, and nine-year-old Michael Bryan. The foster-children lived with the invalid Alfred Walton and his wife in a bungalow a few hundred yards away.

It was just as the children's programme ended that the Beckertons' son Peter came in. A keen sailor, he had been spending his Saturday afternoon as usual, pottering on the beach. The sea was coming over the bank, he reported.

The two men, father and son, decided to go to the Waltons' bungalow and bring the couple, who were in their sixties, and had a third foster-child

Mrs Vera Beckerton (left) returns to the wreckage of her bungalow at Snettisham. It was from here that her son, Peter Beckerton, set out on a vain errand of mercy which led to his death. The three dogs were also flood survivors. *Mrs Vera Beckerton, B.E.M.*

with them, back. As soon as they got outside, it was clear that the situation was worsening rapidly, but they struggled on. When the sea-water reached their waists, Peter shouted to his father to go back, while he went on to the Waltons'. Frederick Beckerton battled home. Taking a last look towards the Waltons' bungalow, he saw Peter a few yards from their door. It must have been only seconds after that that the surge carried Peter Beckerton and the Waltons' bungalow away. When Peter's body was found six weeks later, his watch was stuck at 6.20. His effort, which gained him a posthumous Albert Medal, had been in vain: both the Waltons were drowned, together with their third foster-child.

Meanwhile, back at home, Frederick Beckerton found that the sea had already crashed through the verandah doors. He tried to wedge furniture against them to keep them closed, while, like other flood victims, his wife made an absurd but instinctive resort to brushes and brooms, with which she armed the children. But there was not keeping the sea out, and adults and children retreated to the kitchen. Mrs Beckerton remembers lining the children up against the door to keep it open, realising that if it closed and were held fast by the water there would be no escape for any of them.

In fact, their one chance of escape was just outside—their thirty-year-old ten-foot lugsail, which Peter had been planning to repair and re-paint. With sheets snatched from the linen-cupboard, Mrs Beckerton went outside and lashed the boat fast. Then, with the water chest-high by this time, the Beckertons helped the children into the boat one by one. It was the beginning of a seven-hour ordeal. While the children bailed with cake-tins, the Beckerton parents stood up to their necks in water to keep the lugsail afloat in the poor shelter provided by the shattered bungalow. Timber and furniture cannoned into them as it swept past on the surge. They saw a complete bungalow sail past. A bicycle was hurled into the boat and hastily tossed out by Mr Beckerton. His widow, now in her seventies, tells the story with a kind of wry wonder, almost as if she cannot believe that all this happened to her. But it was real enough, and from time to time she still wakes screaming in the night.

It was in this area that the 7.27 p.m. train from Hunstanton to Lynn, steam-hauled along the single-track line laid on an embankment across the marshes, collided with a floating bungalow. About half-way between Hunstanton and Heacham, the train was met by a huge wave with the bungalow travelling on its crest. The building "struck the engine squarely on the smoke-box and damaged the vacuum brake pipe, so that the engine became immovable". The lights failed, the engine fire went out, chunks of debris battered the stricken train, and passengers had to stand on the seats to keep clear of the water. "For six hours the engine-men and the guard kept up the morale of the passengers, and at length succeeded in affecting temporary repairs to the brakes and, by using the floor-boards of the tender as fuel, in raising sufficient steam to propel slowly back to Hunstanton."

By mid-evening, awareness of the danger was spreading along the north Norfolk coast. At Blakeney, ten miles east of Wells, H. H. Rich was driving home to the coastal village of Cley and noticed that flood boards were being put up, but it was not until his son, returning from a trip into Cley village, told him of the advance of the sea that he registered the need to do something. "So we ripped up a bit of the stair-carpet and got the dining-room carpet upstairs," Mr Rich wrote in an account two days later. "I then had a look and found the water up the drive towards the front door. I unscrewed the door from the store-box in the larder with an idea of using it as a flood board. It took under five minutes, but by the time I got it to the front door the water was in.

We dashed into the sitting-room and got some of the rugs on to chairs. Then the front door went and we waded about salvaging some food. Then the lights went, followed very quickly by the north-facing door. We went upstairs, with the water reaching the fourth stair and the waves breaking through the windows. There was nothing left for it but to go to bed.

We lay down in our clothes in our room after knotting some sheets together to get out of the back window in case the front of the house collapsed. It was then only about eight o'clock. Everything had happened very quickly."

All along the north Norfolk coast, people were making an effort to save their most precious possessions and climbing upstairs to save themselves, though most were to have a less restful night than the unruffled Mr Rich, who "had a very good sleep and didn't wake up until the alarm went". Madeleine Swinn, in Wells, tried to retrieve some linen from the ottoman in her front room—and dropped an armful into the water. At Marsh Farm, Burnham Norton, a sow with a new litter was ensconced on a floating sofa before the farmer and his family withdrew to the first floor; sow and litter were found safe and well, still on the sofa, when the waters receded. Geese were collected and taken to safety in sacks. Cats lived up to their reputation and fended for themselves, finding refuge on cushions or chests of drawers above water level. Perhaps surprisingly, pigs proved to come not far behind cats when it came to the survival instinct. In Lincolnshire, one pig made capital out of the situation by taking refuge on a potato clamp, where it enjoyed a virtually limitless supply of food and burrowed down to the straw to find a bed, only being discovered, well-fed and well-rested, when the waters had gone down and the farm was reoccupied.

But it was the suddenness with which the sea struck, combined with the fact that it happened after dark, that lent added terror to what was already the wildest of wild nights. And consistently, all round the east coast, the eventual

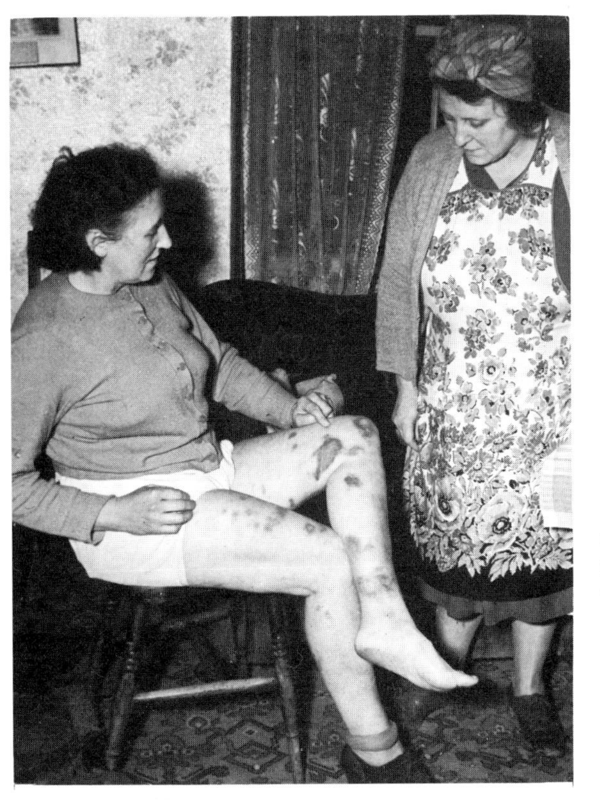

Mrs Vera Beckerton shows her sister some of the injuries she received during her seven hours in the water, buffeted by floating debris.
East Midland Allied Press

death-tolls showed that it was the elderly, who went to bed early and had meagre reserves of energy even if they had time to realise what was happening when the water hit them, who were most vulnerable. The average age of the thirty-five dead in Clacton's bungalow suburb of Jaywick was sixty-six. Five of the eight drowned at Harwich were over sixty. Many old people who escaped the first onslaught died as a result of the shock, exposure and trials that followed. For those who took rescue duties upon themselves, and more especially those with responsibility for elderly relatives, the helplessness and bewilderment of the old added to the night's burdens. At Snettisham, villagers who had organised a rescue party to evacuate the beach settlement saw old people swept out of their arms on the current, within yards of safety, while one local resident sat helpless in his stalled car while water overwhelmed two elderly people in a van twenty yards in front of him. At Old Farm, Salthouse, another coastal village near Wells, Margaret Cooke, her mother, an uncle and two brothers were having a late tea when water "quite suddenly" started to come in at the door. They went upstairs, but the water pursued them there, too. They retreated again, this time to the roof space. There was no skylight, and they were eventually rescued by rope from a hole smashed in the tiles.

Between 8.30 p.m. and 9 p.m., the surge rounded the north-east corner of Norfolk, battering the cliffs with which this area is edged. From Witton, H. Grantham-Hill set out in his car to see what had happened to the cliff-top house, The Hermitage at Bacton, in which he had lived until the previous summer. (As it turned out, it was not until the next dav that he found out: the twenty-one yards of cliff between the house and the sea had vanished, taking the garage, a very large one according to Mr Grantham-Hill, with it.) It was a nightmare journey. "I first had to avoid some dangling telephone wires and haystacks over the road," Mr Grantham-Hill remembers. Beyond the Ship Inn, he stopped to look at a house on the cliff edge that was in obvious danger. "It was already completely engulfed, out to sea, and flashing continually from shorting electricity cables. I was told that no one was in danger. I looked over the cliff, with which I was very familiar, and could see that the sea was hitting high up against it in a manner that I had never seen before—not straight on, but sweeping down from the north-west and taking large chunks off all the time."

Driving south towards Walcott Gap, Mr Grantham-Hill "suddenly realised that the wet was more than rain and that I was driving in sea. I reversed, and then drove round other roads to approach Walcott from the other side. I left my car some way from the sea, and went to locate the one local policeman. He told me that he had evacuated all the people in possible danger, so I went back to my car and found that the sea had just reached it. I had to start it on the handle, with the sea gaining. I went back home exhausted, as much from standing against the wind as anything".

A Kings Lynn school becomes a temporary rest centre, and survivors, wearing borrowed clothes, re-live the terrors of the night.

South of Happisburgh, the cliffs end and the coastline returns to dunes near the village of Sea Palling. There was a whist drive that night in the Nissen hut that served Sea Palling as its village hall. Kathleen Deary, who still lives in the village, was there. The drive came to an abrupt halt when the vicar arrived with the news that the sea was coming through. At once, the village people dispersed to fling themselves into rescue operations. Mrs Deary remembers her father, a man over six feet tall, lifting a baby calf on to his shoulders and leading his herd of cows to safety. But Sea Palling suffered badly, seven village people being drowned. One of two ladies over seventy who had to flee to the roof of their bungalow died of exposure. One family lost both its children—an elder daughter who, having finished delivering the evening papers, went home to her death, and a baby who was swept off her father's back as he struggled with her through the water. Two elderly sisters escaped to the bank, but one slipped off into the water. The landlord of the Life Boat Inn, which was literally engulfed by the sea, was drowned trying to reach a rescue boat.

Still in Sea Palling, Florence Ridley was getting supper for her parents and a friend of the family who was staying with them when Mary Grapes, a farmer's daughter from the other side of the village, called to say that the sea had come over. This was about 8.30 p.m. Florence's father and Eva, the friend of the family, went out to see for themselves what was happening, and a little later, hearing what sounded like cries of help from across the road, Florence and her mother followed.

"We got to the garden gate," Florence Ridley remembers, "when a huge wave simply came up to us, bowling us back into the bungalow. I managed to get Mum inside. We could see the sea sweeping across our garden. We saw the hedge go under, and then the fence beyond. All was one great sheet of water, hissing and roaring its way over the fields.

Dad said we must get out or we would be pinned up against the ceiling. I put a thick coat on Mum, then a mackintosh, and wrapped her head up well and put on her wellies. Eva did the same and Dad and I got ourselves well coated." Miss Ridley's father wedged a ladder so that they could reach the roof.

Just then our nearest neighbours came through the back door, an old lady about eighty and her daughter, who was, I suppose, in her forties. With the doors open back and front, the water just roared through, catching up and sweeping away the furniture. My poor Mum said just one sentence: 'My poor home, all my home.' After that she was silent as though numb.

Dad and I got the two older women up the ladder, Dad going up first to help them up. I pushed them up the ladder with my head. It was pretty hard, as the wind was tearing past at a great rate and the sea was rising rapidly all the time. Then we got Eva up, which was difficult because she was in a plaster cast owing to a slipped disc. Then I followed. We got ourselves all huddled by the chimney-stack, holding one another on as the roof was wet, slippery and I suspect a bit icy."

For the Ridleys and their neighbours, it was the beginning of a five-and-a-half hour wait. "I watched the water still rising and was in fear of us all being swept off the roof. We saw animals, trees and large objects float by. We saw the lights of the village and what we thought was a bus making its way along the main road. At last, after what seemed a lifetime, the water receded and we could see the roof of a house appear in the distance. Dad decided our best plan was to get down and inside, if only to get out of the driving rain and wind."

It was 9 p.m. — an hour before high water — when water began to rise in the streets of Great Yarmouth. In Lichfield Road Jack Loveday, like other householders earlier on the more northerly coasts, tried at first to rig up some temporary barrier at his door. But with the River Yare, about a quarter of a mile away, bursting its banks, the force of the water was too strong for temporary expedients of that kind. "We began to take portable items of furniture upstairs, as well as food and water," Mr Loveday remembers. "Then the electricity failed, but we continued to work by the light of an oil lamp and candles. Soon the water was in all the downstairs rooms and the fire hissed out. The water, due to the fact that the house was built at the highest part of the street, eventually stopped at the third stair tread." With their daughter Anita, then five months old, the Lovedays spent the night sleeping fitfully upstairs, comforted by having checked the time of high water in the *Yarmouth Mercury* and realising that after midnight the water should begin to go down. Their main worry was whether, in the morning, they would be able to boil a kettle for the baby's feed.

Others in Great Yarmouth were less fortunate. Behind the town stretches the five-mile-long gooseneck of Breydon Water, well-known to thousands of

Broads holidaymakers. That night, the banks of Breydon Water gave way, attacking from the rear the town that was already battered from the sea in front. Nine Yarmouth people died, and some ten thousand had to be evacuated from their homes.

In Lowestoft, a few miles to the south, Detective-Constable Allenby Sparkes came off evening duty with his friend Detective-Constable R. G. Daniels and strolled down to the Royal Hotel for a drink. "As we crossed the swing bridge," Mr Sparkes remembers, "I remarked that the tide was 'rather high' but attached no importance to the fact that the water was only a foot or two below the level of the road.

When we had been in the hotel for about half an hour, the lights went out suddenly and then came on again. Somebody said that the road outside was awash with water, and there was a scramble to get out. We were carried along with the crowd, and when we got outside we could see that the road was several feet deep in water.

I'phoned the station and was told that calls for help had been heard coming from St John's Church nearby, and would we investigate and do what we could to help."

The cries came from a party of some forty children, with adult helpers, who had been to a social in the church hall and, when the water rose, had been led by the verger into the darkened church for shelter. At first, they had stayed near the door, but as the water rose further they were forced further back. By the time the two detectives arrived, with a uniformed constable who had received a similar instruction, the refugees were marooned above the altar steps, with the aisle waist-deep in water and the pews adrift in it.

The policemen had had to wade through chest-high water to reach the church, and the uniformed constable had to dive under the water to turn the door-handle. Fortunately, Mr Sparkes had a torch—the only light in the

The train now marooned at platform one . . . A scene at Yarmouth's South Town station.
Press Association

building that was working—but there was nothing for it but to wait for rescue, doing what the police could to keep the shocked women and children calm. Earlier, the verger and a children's entertainer who had been hired for the evening had conducted children's singing from the piano in the nave, but as the water level crept up they had had to abandon their position.

After about half an hour, local boatman Reggie Stigles turned up. He tried to row up the aisle but was unable to do so owing to the obstruction caused by the driving pews. "By this time," says Mr Sparkes, "my colleagues and I were beginning to show signs of cold through our immersion in the water, and I told the others to get into the boat to be taken over the bridge. Then I started to carry the children one by one from the altar steps to the boat until it was full, and then waited for its return, when I repeated the process. The boat made about four trips, and I left on the last one. While waiting, I climbed out of the water and on to the altar, but I found that I couldn't stop shaking, so I went back into the water where the cold did not affect me quite so much."

Church member or not, one lady among the rescued seems not to have taken to heart the text about laying up treasure on earth. Mr Sparkes recalls that she had no concern for her companions, least of all the children, but when it was her turn to be carried to the boat "gave me explicit instructions not to get her fur coat wet".

"Had I not been in a House of God," the former detective comments, "I would probably have dropped her into the water and made her walk to the boat."

Meanwhile, at the Suffolk Hotel in London Road, Lowestoft, the annual dinner of the Lowestoft Choral Society was proving unexpectedly eventful. When flood water began to fill the cellars, hotel manager Charles Smith warned the guests that they should leave at once or be prepared to sit it out until the flood went down. Most of them stayed, sitting in the darkness and increasing cold after Mr Smith had pulled the fuses and drawn the boilers. For most of them, the evening out ended at about four in the morning, by which time the water had receded enough for the menfolk to carry their women home.

In fact, Lowestoft, though there was severe damage, got away without any loss of life on land. A few years before, a new sea-wall had been built at a cost which many ratepayers had criticised. But the wall took the full fury of the sea, blunting it so that although the town was flooded it was not overwhelmed with the suddenness that shattered less well-protected places along the coast. If the wall had not held, the town, with Oulton Broad behind it, might well have been trapped between two waters as happened at Great Yarmouth.

But eleven Lowestoft families were nevertheless left to mourn when the storm had abated. On Friday 30th January, a fleet of twelve trawlers had left harbour for the fishing-grounds, among them the *Guava*, skippered by George "Tash" Fisher with a ten-man crew. On Saturday the *Guava* radioed that she

Rescuers at work among the prefabs at Langer Road, Felixstowe, where most of the town's victims died. *East Anglian Daily Times*

was stowing her gear and hoping to dodge the weather. Her position was about half-way between England and Holland. But there was no dodging the weather that night, and the *Guava* was neither seen nor heard of again. Despite an intensive air and sea search, no wreckage or bodies were ever recovered.

Late evening, the havoc was spreading southwards, becoming more deadly as, in the bungalow villages of the Suffolk and Essex coasts, people went to their vulnerable beds. On the coast further north, full-scale rescue operations were by now under way. Shortly after sunset, the sea had broken through at Sutton-on-Sea, Lincolnshire, smashing a 300-yard gap in the dunes—the biggest single breach of the night. The suddenness of this assault made casualties inevitable. Two policemen sent to Sutton-on-Sea to warn local residents had to abandon their mission when they found themselves in water five feet deep, and were themselves cut off for the rest of the night, unable to report on the situation to their base at Mablethorpe because by this time all telephones were out of action. In fact, the whole strip of Lincolnshire coastal villages, in which the death-toll came to forty, was cut off by phone, so that the Mablethorpe police had for several hours to rely on their own meagre resources, having had to evacuate the police station when the Mablethorpe sea-wall collapsed.

The contrast between the fortunes of urban and rural areas was marked. Although Kings Lynn received the full force of the surge, bringing the water a foot higher than the previous record of 1883 and flooding about one-fifth of the town to depths of up to six feet, there were only fifteen deaths, a comparatively light tally considering that 1,800 houses had to be evacuated. As we have seen, Lowestoft escaped with no fatalities, and even Great Yarmouth, trapped between two waters, suffered only nine deaths. All these are, of course, substantial towns, able even on a midwinter Saturday night to muster a sizeable emergency corps composed of police, firemen, ambulance-men, council workmen, and so on, and with enough responsible and knowledgeable people on hand to direct rescue and relief operations. Also, they are towns largely made up of solid two-storey houses. It is significant that the stretches of coast where the casualties were heaviest—the Mablethorpe-Sutton area of Lincolnshire, the Hunstanton-to-Lynn area, Jaywick, Canvey Island—were largely seaside shanty-towns consisting mainly of timber bungalows never intended for winter occupation and with minimal police or other emergency cover. At Felixstowe, most of the forty deaths were on an estate of single storey post-Second World War prefabs. By contrast, an area where the breaching and over-topping of the defences were as bad as anywhere, between Holkham and Wells, escaped without loss of life, a fact attributable to the conservationist policy of the landowner, the fifth Lord Leicester, who had only a year or two before taken steps to remove a budding shanty-type development near Burnham Overy Staithe. There are, however, still many places on the Norfolk, Suffolk and Essex coasts where the warning has not been heeded, and where flimsy dwellings stand exposed to the sea or well below high-water level behind clay banks.

At Snettisham, rescue operations were for several hours maintained by voluntary effort. Mr Temple Cole and his neighbours made innumerable journeys between the beach settlement and the Station Inn, which quickly became a sort of advance medical station. Like Detective-Constable Sparkes in Lowestoft, Mr Temple Cole came across a lady who was concerned for her fur coat. She insisted on going back for it, and it cost her her life; her body, still without the coat, was found next morning in a hedge in the field next to her bungalow.

They were nightmare journeys between the beach and the pub. Mr Temple Cole remembers that, in addition to the difficulty of steering the car through the surging water, there was the wind to be coped with, together with an airborne barrage of straw, hay, branches and other debris. Salt-spray covered the rescuers and their cars, and "to make things more unpleasant it started to snow and sleet for a time".

One of Mr Temple Cole's neighbours, a Mr Whitmore, had served in the Royal Navy throughout the war, but confessed that he had never been so frightened in his life as he was that night. Coming back from the beach with two elderly women, his car stalled in the flood. "Gradually the water came higher and higher, and the car rocked from side to side, and each moment they expected to end up in the ditch. As the water crept even higher up their legs, the two men in front sat on the backs of the seats with their feet on the seats, and the two ladies in the back seat sat on the back ledge, all with their backs doubled up under the roof. Finally the lights failed, and the water began to flow through the windows, so they opened them in the hope that they would have less resistance to the water. They began to think that they would have to try to climb out and haul each other on to the roof." But the water was checked, and then began to recede slowly, and after two hours trapped inside the car, much of that time spent in a crouching position under the roof, Mr Whitmore, his companion and the two women were carried to safety.

While Mr Temple Cole continued his shuttle service to and from the beach, his wife set up a sort of private rest centre for some of the rescued and evacuated people, at the same time ringing round to friends organising a car pool for further rescue work. Again and again Mr Temple Cole returned with victims and to change his sodden clothes. "I was upheld that night," he commented later, "by my despised habit of hoarding old clothes and refusing all permission to part with them for jumble sales." As a result, he was able to find at least five changes.

Eventually, police arrived from neighbouring villages and took over the organisation of the evacuation. But for the local rescuers, the work went on, each incident of that long night one which, in normal times, would have merited an award for bravery; and the more remarkable because people so quickly adapted themselves to circumstances beyond their experience or wildest expectations. As far as Mr Temple Cole was concerned, the night's novelties included dialling 999 for the first time in his life ("the service was amazingly swift", he remembers) to "wading in cold, dirty salt water about half-way up my thighs whilst wearing only short knee-length gumboots, which were of course all the time full of water, carrying an unconscious woman on my back".

Out at Snettisham beach, the ordeal of the Beckertons continued. It was well past midnight when the water began to recede—not that this improved the family's position for a time, because they now had to fight against the flow of the tide in the opposite, and potentially even more hazardous, direction. But the, Vera Beckerton remembers, quite suddenly the sea had gone and they found themselves on a shingle bank. Among the debris nearby was a trunk which proved to contain blankets—wet, but still better than nothing. Wrapping each child in one, the Beckertons settled the children down on the shingle while they considered what to do next. Uppermost in their minds was the thought of the next tide. Although they had lost all track of time, they knew that the turn could not be far away.

Then they saw a light shining in the distance. Mrs Beckerton's first thought was that it was her son Peter; she was not to know that he had died several hours earlier. In fact, the light came from a search party led by Snettisham's policeman, Henry Nobbs, who had been continually at work since dusk and had several hours' duty still ahead of him. When the water retreated,

Mrs Vera Beckerton, B.E.M., with the five children for whose rescue she was awarded the Medal. Beside her is her adopted daughter Hazel; the others are Michael Beckerton (nine), Shirley Baxter (eleven), John Beckerton (seven) and Michael Bryan (nine).
East Midland Allied Press

it left a waist-high lake in the pits behind the shingle bank. P. C. Nobbs, with a party of helpers, resorted to a tactic he had already employed to good effect earlier that night — a rope line — and led the Beckerton party and eleven other victims to dry land. It was the coming together of two of Snettisham's local heroes, soon to be recognised nationally. Both Vera Beckerton and Henry Nobbs were awarded the British Empire Medal, two of seventeen subsequently awarded for that night's work.

One of the pleasant surprises of the night in the Hunstanton area was the swift and effective reaction to the disaster of the U.S. Air Force. "The Yanks" were not particularly popular in north-west Norfolk. Chauvinist resentment bred in wartime still made itself felt; in addition, American servicemen seemed ostentatiously prosperous in an area traditionally one of Britain's poorest. They rented as married quarters homes (in which some of them, indeed, were to die on the night of the flood) that local people felt should have been used for local needs. They created a brisk vice trade at King's Lynn and even in genteel Hunstanton. But on the night of 31st January 1953, while the meagre civilian front-line forces of police, council workers and volunteers were doing their brave but painfully inadequate best and British officialdom was refusing to be nudged out of its weekend torpor, the U.S.A.F. showed a foreign and welcome readiness to cut corners, identify immediate needs and *act*.

It was, of course, not an effort devoid of self-interest. Many U.S.A.F. men and their families lived on the stricken stretch of coast between Hunstanton and Lynn; the memorial at South Beach, Hunstanton, alone lists sixteen Americans among the thirty-one victims named. But nevertheless, inside an hour of the disaster units from the base at Sculthorpe, several miles inland, were on the scene, and not only looking after their own. To those reared in the British tradition of somnolent officialdom, this was a revelation.

"I don't know if they suffer from red tape," the Hunstanton coroner said at the inquest on thirty-two of the victims, speaking of the Americans at Sculthorpe and hinting at a grievance that was already being expressed about official British reaction to the flood; "If they do, the commander ignored it completely. Within an hour they arrived with equipment, men and detachments . . . Our American friends will leave behind an enduring memory of courage and assistance in these troubled times."

The American forces, having been among the first helpers from outside the area to arrive at the disaster scene, followed up later with field kitchens to succour the volunteer rescuers and returning householders and, a grimmer task, with parties of beachcombers working methodically along the shoreline in search of bodies. But the American effort is not to be written off as merely institutional, the reaction of an army of occupation aware of possible public relations angles. One of the heroes of the night, later to be the first non-British

Enfield Highway
Library
Hertford Road
Enfield 443-2300

recipient of the George Medal, was U.S.A.F. Corporal Reis Leming, based at Sculthorpe. Leming, then twenty-two and a non-swimmer, single-handedly rescued twenty-seven people from the South Beach area of Hunstanton, alternately shoving or drifting with his rubber dinghy among the shattered bungalows, until, after four hours, he collapsed from exposure.

Meanwhile, over at Sea Palling, the water was beginning to recede, leaving furniture, trees, animals and the general bric-a-brac of disaster trapped on walls and in hedges. But the ordeal of the Ridley family was not yet over, though they had now climbed down from the roof. They were all suffering from exposure—especially the old lady from next door, whom they laid on a table and tried to keep warm by rubbing her hands.

"Just then, three or four men from the village came in. They took the old lady away with them and told us to 'Get out, keep under the hills (the dunes) and keep right.'

As we struggled along I realised that the hills had been washed away and we must indeed keep right. We fell into holes, we stumbled against objects in our way, and the water was lapping around our waists. It was terrifying. My Dad had suffered a major stroke—I was worried about him and kept calling him. He answered once or twice and then he was silent. I found out afterwards that he had found a boat and thrown himself in, thinking all was lost. He was found later, in a sorry state but safe.

Mum—silent—was trying her best to get her feet to move, but she was getting tired and weak. I had to lift each foot up and place it down, so that our progress was slow. Our wellies were filling with sand, and as each step was taken it was heavier than the last. As I bent down to lift Mum's feet up, the water came through my clothing and out at the throat. It was a terrible, terrible fight for our lives." It says something for the depth of Florence Ridley's experience that the detailed account from which I have quoted so extensively was written twenty-one years later.

"We had lost Eva," her story goes on. "She had started out with us, and we found out later that a man had come to her aid when she had cried out for fear of being sucked down. After a long time some men appeared, and one took my Mum. I let her go and knew no more. I came to my senses to find that I had been carried down to our local pub, which had become the rescue centre." There Florence, her parents and Eva were re-united, having cheated death more times in one night than most people can expect to have to do in the course of a lifetime—though Florence's parents, she says, never recovered from the night of the flood, despite living on for a number of years: "They lost their hold on living then. They had lost their home, and the new one we built up did not seem the same."

The darkness, the urgency of the immediate rescue operations and the essentially local nature of these efforts in a sparsely-populated area all tended to conceal the true scale of the disaster that had struck the east coast that night. As a farmer's wife at Holkham told me, "We thought we were the only ones". It was not until the next morning that most people realised that the sea had struck beyond their own village or street. And this was as true of officials as of farmers' wives. One official commentator noted that "during the night such alarming reports kept coming in that many thought darkness and uncertainty had magnified the disaster. However, when daylight came it was found that darkness had in fact hidden much of the damage and that things were far worse than could have been imagined".

The first troops, with airmen from the R.A.F. and U.S.A.F. bases with which East Anglia was then still thickly dotted, started to move to the coastal areas during the night, ostensibly to help seal the breaches in the sea defences before the next tide. In the event, they found that there was more urgent work to be done first, rescuing families still cut off, ferrying the rescued to hospitals and rest centres, and in Yarmouth, according to one report, providing a reassuring presence against looting.

But there had been no let-up for those who were on the scene first. In Kings Lynn, Bertie Hart was still at work. He had been touring the town, helping where he could. He drove to the police station to summon help to Diamond Street where, he had been told, there were bodies floating in the water—a police matter. This area of Lynn had caught the full force of the flood, and local people had had only a few moments to get out of their homes. Fifteen people failed to reach safety. Then Mr Hart went to South Lynn, a pig-keeping area where dead beasts were littering the place. "One dear old man called us to ask if we could remove a dead pig that had been washed through his living-room window as it was upsetting his wife," Mr Hart recalls. "We went to have a look-see, but it was too heavy for us to move, so we had to leave it until more help came." It was 4.30 a.m. when Mr Hart finally gave up for the night and went home.

About the same time, Mr Temple Cole at Snettisham also decided to call it a night. "The real heroes of the night," he said later, "were undoubtedly just ordinary people—the village copper, the plumber, the electrician, three or four farmers or sons of farmers, a couple of Red Cross men (later) and one or two firemen. They all did a jolly fine job under conditions which, up till then, I would have been certain that it would be impossible to stand."

The unexpected reserves of courage, determination and resource miraculously released in ordinary people by disaster had saved many lives that night. But as the waters retreated across the marshes, hissing and bubbling and snickering as they went, the tideline revealed that for some—the woman who had gone back for her fur coat, a baby girl who, to the farm worker who found her body some days later, looked like a doll, the Sea Palling couple literally sucked out of their bedroom when the front wall of their house collapsed into the sea — disaster had come too swiftly and cruelly to be entirely cheated of victims. Meanwhile, as Saturday turned into Sunday and January 1953 into February, there were still lives to be snatched in the sleeping towns and villages of the Suffolk and Essex coast.

U.S. servicemen from Langham Camp help out at Salthouse, north Norfolk, where furniture and belongings from shattered homes were taken to the village church, on a hilltop, for safe keeping. *Press Association*

CHAPTER THREE

AS SATURDAY became Sunday, the surge moved on. The sky had cleared by now, the squalls of the early evening giving way to bright moonlight, but the north-westerly winds persisted. From Norfolk the surge was running southwards at a height of eight feet towards the Dutch coast, about two hours ahead of high tide. In front of the surge itself, water from the previous outgoing tide which had been prevented from getting away was seeping back into the coastal inlets, providing a residue of water on which surge and tide were to build in the forthcoming hours.

South of Lowestoft, as far as Felixstowe, run some fifty miles of low-lying coastline consisting largely of sand and shingle beaches punctuated by the estuaries of the Rivers Blyth, Ore and Deben. The two major coastal towns are Southwold and Aldeburgh, the only two survivors among a dozen or more settlements which were of some importance up to Saxon times, but which have since been claimed by the sea. Today, the Sizewell nuclear power station and the huge radar installation at Orfordness are among the most prominent features of this coastal strip, but in 1953 the area's remoteness and lack of population had made it ideal for gunnery ranges, bombing-practice areas, the R.A.F. early-warning station at Bawdsey, and other such installations.

The gales of the previous twenty-four hours had already wrought havoc with telephone and power lines in this area, and among the few people on the road that Saturday night were a number of Eastern Electricity Board engineers, repairing overhead lines. Another was Dr Blyth, of Southwold, out on an emergency call. His wife Vivien, pregnant with her third child, was awaiting her husband's return.

"Our red setter came in, shaking with terror, and crawled into a minute space under a chair," Mrs Blyth remembers. It was her first intimation of anything out of the ordinary. "An hour or so later my husband strode in. 'The tide is over the sea-wall,' he said in a dramatic voice. 'Southwold is an island. People are drowning. I shall be out all night.' He donned warm sweaters, boots and so on and left, not to return till next day."

"My immediate thoughts were totally selfish," says Mrs Blyth. "Supposing I went into labour? I had a bed booked at Halesworth Cottage Hospital (ten miles away) but no traffic could cross the bridge."

As it turned out, her fears were groundless; her baby was not born until three weeks later. But Southwold—like so many small coastal places, approached by road from the surrounding area by only one route—was indeed cut off. The flood water running ahead of the surge, sweeping round the town from north and south in a pincer movement, had marooned the little town in a sea stretching from Reydon in the north to Wenhaston in the east. Apart from a shuttle service operated by a tractor and trailer, which was used to ferry sandbags and other essential supplies, Southwold was to remain cut off for forty-eight hours.

At Ferry Road, Southwold, was one of the piecemeal developments characteristic of the English coastline: timber-framed bungalows intended as summer holiday homes but in some cases occupied permanently, often by elderly people. As in north-west Norfolk, in Lincolnshire, and further south at Jaywick and Canvey Island, such buildings were to prove death-traps that night. At Southwold, about thirty of these bungalows were seriously damaged, some being totally wrecked in the first onslaught of the sea and others being picked up and carried along bodily until they were dashed to pieces against obstructions.

In one of the bungalows in Ferry Road lived the Sorick family from U.S.A.F. Bentwaters, with their seven-month-old baby. The Soricks had had two couples from the base over for supper and drinks that night. The convivial occasion was suddenly interrupted when the flood water picked up their bungalow and carried it 400 yards across the marshes. The six adults managed to clamber up on to the roof with the baby, but it was several hours before local lifeboatman "Mobbs" Mayhew, with his friend William Stannard as

A pathetic tangle of wreckage in the Ferry Road area of Southwold, where five residents — three elderly women, and a mother and her four-year-old son — were drowned.

East Anglian Daily Times

crew, managed to locate and rescue the stranded party with the help of car headlights. Mr Mayhew, who was seventy-four at the time, was later awarded the British Empire Medal.

Meanwhile, taxi-driver Jimmy Thomson from Halesworth had dropped a late evening fare in Southwold and was driving back home along the Blackwater road. It was nearly ten o'clock when he saw in his headlights moving water ahead of him. Hastily, he turned his car round and raced back towards Southwold, hoping to get to higher ground. When he reached the crown of the bridge on the town's only link road, he decided to stop and sit out the flood there. He was rescued ten hours—and thirty cigarettes—later.

There was a lucky escape, too, for an Eastern Electricity Board van crew who were caught up in the same onrush of water near Southwold bridge. They sat it out for a while, but when the water reached headlight level they decided to abandon the vehicle, one wading to safety while the other clambered along railings and walls. Seconds after they left the van, it was swept off the road and ended up with its front wheels in a ditch and the cab completely submerged.

Southwold had one ambulance, operated by the Red Cross, and it was already on its way to the scene of the disaster in Ferry Road. Driving it was sixty-year-old W. G. Easthaugh, with barber Frank Hurr in the passenger seat. On the way to Ferry Road, the going became increasingly hard. Eventually, they ran into rubble and shingle, and the ambulance, caught by the wind and tide, turned over. Mr Easthaugh climbed out and, wading waist-high, found an unoccupied bungalow with a verandah. Smashing a window to get in, he remained there for six hours until the tide turned. His mate, Frank Hurr, had meanwhile gone for help when the ambulance stopped, but found himself trapped. Caught by the surge of water, Mr Hurr grabbed a baulk of timber and held on to it as it was swept across the marsh. His nightmare journey ended when he fetched up with the current on rising ground, where he was later found by a local policeman.

Further south, the coastal village of Dunwich was well-used to the assault of the sea which, as mentioned in Chapter One, has been eating away at the land at this point for centuries. Dorothy Jay, Dunwich's voluntary local historian, remembers that on the night of Saturday 31st January "there was a bright full moon and a very strong north-westerly gale, and by 11.30 p.m. water was very high on the marshes at the back of the village street". At the lower end of the village, near the church and school, the water level began to rise dangerously. Living in a downstairs room of the school house was a ninety-one-year-old invalid, Mrs Bottomly, who refused to be moved. "It was only when the sea reached the level of the bed," Mrs Jay recalls, "that Special Constables Fred Brewer and George Canham forced their way into the room and took her upstairs. Because of the force of the water, they were unable to open the door and had to climb in the window."

Ten miles south of Dunwich, at Aldeburgh, local butcher Alan Aldridge listened to the end of "Saturday Night Theatre" on the radio and stepped out of his shop door to look at the night. It was, he noted, windy but bright. Suddenly, as he stood looking at the sky, a man and a boy ran past, shouting about the sea coming in at Slaughden, to the south of the town. At first, Mr Aldridge didn't quite catch what they were saying—but he soon understood because, behind them, he saw a wave rolling along the street. Pausing to shutter his shopfront, he rushed round the back to the old slaughter-house where he kept his chickens. Water was already lapping at the door. He clambered in and quickly tidied up, moving the chickens to shelves high off the floor, hanging his guns from the highest hooks he could find, and taking a last quick double-check that everything was safe.

Slaughden, near Aldeburgh, where the only building left standing when the surge retreated was the concrete mine-store seen here still battered by the seas on Sunday. Ironically, materials for new sea defences at Slaughden had already been delivered when the sea struck.

East Anglian Daily Times

That double-check nearly cost Mr Aldridge his life. Turning back to the door, he found that it was held fast by the weight of water outside. Using all his strength, with his shoulder to the door, he managed to open the crack wide enough to slip through as the water rushed in behind him. Back in the house, he retreated to the first floor with half a bottle of whisky to keep out the cold and damp. The tidemarks inside the old slaughter-house when the water had receded showed that the flood had almost reached the ceiling; Mr Aldridge had been no more than a few seconds away from certain death. And it would have been in vain, because most of the chickens had been drowned and even his guns, Mr Aldridge said later, were never the same again.

About two hours to midnight; the rivers and creeks of the Suffolk and Essex coasts were filling up fast. From the police hut at Orfordness, an R.A.F. policeman made what he described as "the last call from the island". Everyone else had left, and he and his mate were going to climb on to the roof of the hut and wait for rescue. At the receiving end of the call was Reginald Partridge, who set out with his brother Francis and two other boatmen for the hut. On the way, they met bales of hay which fouled the engine, and it was 2 a.m. before they reached the hut, which by then had water lapping at its roof.

By this time, the sea had struck its next major blow, and at an unexpected spot. At the west end of Felixstowe, facing inland, the wall lining the estuary of the River Orwell gave way in a number of places, sending a wave of water across the marshes towards the area of Langer Road.

On the corner of Langer Road and Orford Road was a colony of post-war prefabs which caught the full force of the water. Every one of them was moved from its original site, some by as much as two hundred yards. In Stour Avenue, William Leggett awoke to find his house creaking and rocking on its foundations. Looking out he saw water everywhere; the only thing to do was to swim for it. "I half swam and was half taken by the current," he said later. "I could hear my neighbours shouting and screaming but there was nothing I could do. When I looked round, my house was following me down the road. I've been under machine-gun fire during the war, but this was far more frightening."

Eventually, Mr Leggett scrambled up the fire escape of a pub and tried to rouse the landlord. He smashed his way in with a bottle fished out of the water, and it was only with difficulty that he persuaded the occupants that he wasn't a burglar.

In Langer Road, engine fitter Charles Durrant awoke with a start.

"I could hear something gurgling," he said later, "so I got up and looked out of the window towards the railway line. All I could see was just a sheet of water. I shouted to my missus, 'Quick, it looks as if it's going to be a flood' and we both put on dressing-gowns and rushed to the children. Then I could see water suddenly pouring up through the floor."

Felixstowe seafront on Sunday morning. *East Anglian Daily Times*

With his wife and two young children, Mr Durrant scrambled up on to the flat roof via the baby's high chair and the front porch. Their seven-year-old daughter was petrified with fright and couldn't make the climb; eventually the Durrants put her in a box which happened to float by and pulled it to the roof.

"After a struggle," Mr Durrant's story goes on, "I pulled my wife, who was expecting a baby, on to the roof too. We got up by the chimney, on the lee side from the wind, my wife sheltering the girl and I had the boy inside my dressing-gown. I managed to grab some bits of plywood floating by and put them over my wife for shelter . . . We all huddled on the roof, wringing wet. I didn't know what to think. Everything was so quiet, with the moon shining down, I wondered if the end of the world had come." It was about five hours before the Durrants, literally frozen stiff by this time, were rescued by boat. "They dragged us off the roof by our ankles," Mr Durrant remembers. "I don't think I could have stuck it another half an hour."

At Felixstowe's Cavendish Hotel, there had been an old-time dance that Saturday night. Almost before the fug had cleared, the ballroom was to open up again in a different guise—as a rest centre. At the Ritz Cinema, a film called "Night Without Sleep", starring Gary Merrill and Linda Darnell, had been trailered among forthcoming attractions . . .

At Gas Works Cottages, a couple of hundred yards from Langer Road, Violet Sparrow tucked her three children into bed, said goodnight to her husband Eric, who had been called out as an auxiliary coastguard, and went to bed herself. She was not to know that it would be her last night in that house.

About midnight she heard what she thought was the noise of someone breaking in. She went down to check the front door, and it felt as if someone were pushing from the other side. Then, "the door flung open and I was submerged in water up to my neck."

"I got back upstairs," she said afterwards, "and hammered on the wall to warn my neighbours. They shouted back that their house was flooded. We knocked a hole in the wall, which was made of hardboard, and they came into our house. The water was getting deeper and deeper, and when it got to eight inches deep in the bedroom we banged a hole in the ceiling and climbed into the loft. There we stayed, perched on the rafters, until Sunday lunchtime."

In the taller houses along Langer Road, people were awakened by the screams of the prefab-dwellers struggling to reach the relative safety of their rooftops. The Hillary family, living in a flat opposite the prefabs, watched with horror as the prefabs swept by. "As one floated past we saw a woman washed off it," Mrs Hillary said later. "One little girl and her father clung to the roof from half-past twelve until they were rescued at seven o'clock on Sunday morning."

As the final casualty list of thirty-nine names was to show, there was a heavy toll of life, not restricted to the aged or infirm, on the prefab estate, and several whole families died: thirty-year-old Norman Bushnall, his wife Jean, their two-year-old son Keith and six-month-old daughter Brenda; Jack Salmon, his wife Stella and eight-year-old Robin; Frederick and Annie Flather and their two daughters, Janet (seven) and Suzanne (four); Raymond and Sheila Pettitt, their son Brian (six) and two-year-old daughter Gillian; William and Stella Damant and their son Keith. Mothers and children, too: Iris Sadd and four-year-old Patricia; Muriel Allery and four-year-old Jane; Joan Tong and six-year-old Angela. It took over an hour for the relatives of the dead to tramp through the coroner's court at Felixstowe Town Hall on the following Tuesday, giving evidence of identification, though before this ordeal they had to listen to tributes and encomiums from civil dignitaries.

The joint estuaries of the Orwell and the Stour separate Suffolk from Essex. On the north side is Felixstowe; on the south, Harwich. Eight feet above normal, the tide swept into parts of the old town area of Harwich, killing eight people and driving over 1,000 more from their homes. But the comparatively light death-toll is significant; the flooded houses were mainly of the older type, many with basements which absorbed much of the flood water.

The morning after in Main Road, Harwich. *Mrs Marjorie Cocks*

The Wright family from Dovercourt—mother, father and three daughters—had been to Wembley that night to see the pantomime on ice. They arrived back on the coach, Margaret Wright, then fifteen and a half, remembers, about 10.30 p.m. There was as yet no sign of the peril to come, but "just before we reached the top of Manor Road where we lived the wind blew so fiercely it took my eight-year-old sister Josie's breath away, and Mum had to hold her, back to the wind, as we walked along".

Customs officer John Bentley was on late turn that night at the train ferry berth at Harwich. "There was a great deal of paperwork," he remembers, "and at some time, I think about 11 p.m., I found water running into the office. I eventually finished up sitting on the desk and writing between my legs. The job finished, I waded out with my bicycle and went up the road to my home in Dovercourt. The police station was on the way, and I called in there to mention what was going on. I was told that it was under control and I wasn't wanted. I went home. This would be about midnight."

In Albert Street in the Bathside area of Harwich, Mrs A. M. Vincent, living at number three with her husband, a married daughter and her husband and a young baby a few months old, went to bed. Just after midnight, Mrs Vincent's bedroom curtains were snatched from their rail and flung across the room. She got up to see what was happening and looked out of the window.

"There was a wall of water rolling towards us," Mrs Vincent remembers. "It seemed as high as a three-storeyed house. I said, 'Oh God, the sea wall has broken.' We dashed downstairs, calling the family up as we went down. We got nearly to the basement when the bottom stairs just collapsed, so we all stayed on the first floor.

I heard a voice crying 'Save me! Save me!', and up to that time we were so concerned with ourselves that I had completely forgotten my daughter and grandson in the next street. My husband and son-in-law swam from our house to my daughter's flat, only just in time to get them and the other flat-dwellers on to the next floor. I did not see my husband until twelve hours later, so I did not know if he or my daughter had survived."

Meanwhile, customs officer John Bentley had slept badly. After about a couple of hours of fitful rest, he dressed and cycled back into Harwich. "There I found that there was indeed a flood and that rescue services were in operation," he recalls. The police had opened up the town's boating pool and released its dinghies. Mr Bentley took one of these and went to Station Road, where there were people waiting to be rescued from upstairs rooms. The wind was still strong. "At that time I was a very powerful man," he says, "and could row a boat with the best. However, the wind was so strong that I had to make fast to the railings, of which only the top was visible, to avoid being swept away."

Later in the night, still rowing round the town looking for rescue work to be done, Mr Bentley "met a magnificent sight. It was Mr Whelpton, local dentist and character in his own right, and husband of the local R.S.P.C.A. representative. He was rowing a dinghy which was loaded with cats at the stern, dogs in the middle, and a most magnificent parrot perched on the stem and shouting its head off: 'Get out of here, you buggers!'" Before their rescue work was over, the Whelptons were to provide temporary lodging for countless canaries, fourteen dogs and forty-six cats—including one one-eyed and stump-tailed ruffian of a cat which, so they discovered later, was enjoying its

Rescue by boat in Main Road, Harwich. Many of Harwich's flood victims were trapped in the basements of houses like those on the right. The level of water at the height of the flood can be seen on the houses in the background. *Mrs Marjorie Cocks*

Albert Street, Harwich, the morning after the flood. *Mrs A. M. Vincent*

first taste of home life after roughing it for about twelve years as a stray in the streets of Bathside.

In Albert Street, Mrs Vincent's family had discovered the truth of the saying that necessity is the mother of invention. Her daughter's young baby was crying for its 6 a.m. feed, but electricity and gas had long since been cut off. "My son went to the second floor," says Mrs Vincent, "opened the window and grabbed a broken chair that floated by. He took our library books from the bedside and, feeling about in the dark, found his lifeboat matches. We got a nice warm fire going, and kept it up with a regular supply of driftwood. We emptied the hot water bottles into the kettle, boiled it up, and mixed up the feed in the bottom of a soap dish.

By that time I was worried about my parents, both over eighty and living up the road. My son had an old dinghy that he had brought ashore for repair in our backyard, and it had broken loose. He managed to climb out of the second-floor window into it, and found a couple of broomsticks to use as oars. He rowed the whole length of our street, straight up the railway line, and was soon back to tell us that my parents were safe. They had retreated to their top bedrooms and had a candle burning in the window."

Daylight brought rescue for the Bathsiders from the Royal Navy training base at Shotley, but it did not bring Mrs Vincent's worries to an end. She was taken to a temporary rest centre which had been set up at the Alexandra Hotel in Dovercourt, where she overheard a conversation about a Mr Vincent who had been drowned in a bedroom. She had not seen her husband, it will be remembered, since he had set out with her son-in-law for her daughter's flat some hours before. The overheard conversation proved to be a false alarm, but coming on top of the events of the night it put Mrs Vincent into a state of shock from which she took three days to recover.

The Wright family, in Manor Road, Dovercourt, first heard of the floods in Harwich from the B.B.C. morning news. "All thoughts of breakfast went," remembers Margaret, then fifteen, "and I got on my bike. I went into the Barrack Field Hut and will never forget the sad faces of those sitting there, evacuated from their houses and waiting for offers of accommodation."

Margaret's sympathy for the homeless led her into a trap the memory of which can still make her scalp tingle: "Completely shocked at what I saw, and near to tears, I offered accommodation to a family I knew. Surely my mum would have no objection! I raced home on my bike, but the car bearing the flooded-out family arrived first. My mum, not realising what was going on, was explaining that she had no room to spare. I have never, before or since, felt so embarrassed." But all was eventually well: the evacuees were found rooms a few doors up the road.

Harwich police station had been one of the first victims of the flood, and the telephone exchange at Dovercourt was quickly pressed into use as an emergency control centre. Tom Nicholls, whose father was night supervisor at the exchange, remembers that the operators were on duty continuously for thirty-six hours, supplied with hot food by Tom's mother, who lived just round the corner. Tom—at that time living in the Midlands—recalls that it was fourteen hours before he could get through on the telephone to check whether his parents were safe.

South of Harwich, some eight miles of marsh and broken coastline stretch towards Frinton. It is a bleak country whose banks, inlets and marshland were in 1953 relieved only by the 160-acre site of an industrial explosives factory at

The day before the flood, this was a neat row of orderly beach huts lining the front at Dovercourt. *Mrs Marjorie Cocks*

Bramble Island — in fact, a peninsula. On the night of 31st January, there was only one man on duty at the factory — a nightwatchman named Archibald. He had made a check call at midnight to his works manager, but nothing had been heard of him since. At about three o'clock on Sunday morning, Dovercourt lorry-driver Leonard Gostling was awoken by the local policeman and doctor, and asked if he could organise a search.

Mr Gostling dressed, picked up his mate Donald Harris, and went to Dovercourt Sailing Club to collect "the best boat we could find". It was, however, in poor condition, and they went to Mr Harris's house to pick up a baler and rowlocks. By the time they reached Dock Lane, off Bramble Island, the doctor had rounded up an employee at the factory as a guide. But the boat could carry only three, and if the mission were successful and the watchman found it would have been overloaded. So Mr Gostling and Mr Harris set out alone, Mr Harris rowing.

"It was a strong pull," Mr Gostling noted in an account written shortly after the event, "but I could not relieve my mate as the wind would have blown us into the telephone wires. The water was level with them." Seeing light from a garage, they made their way in that direction in the hope of a quick rescue, only to find that the light came from the headlamps of several lorries, turned on when water got at the batteries and circuits. Shortly after this, the boat floundered and the two men had to continue their mission on foot, wading waist-, chest- and even at times neck-high. "I could just walk with my toes on the ground and using my hands in a swimming motion," Mr Gostling recalled later. They reached a point between two lines of factory buildings where baulks of timber, empty oil-drums and other debris made it necessary for them to claw their way through. Slowly, they worked their way through the factory huts, calling into the wind. As they reached the garage again on completing a circuit of the site a fresh torrent of water poured across their path and they had to fight to find a new path round it. When they arrived back, they were all in.

Next morning at daybreak, the local policeman searched again, but found only the watchman's lamp. It was not until six weeks later that the body was washed up at Walton.

To the south, beyond Clacton, lay the bungalow beach settlement of Jaywick. The contrast between the flood's toll here and in Harwich is significant. In Harwich, many of the flooded houses were of the older type with basements which absorbed some of the flood water; at Jaywick, few homes were anything more than holiday or temporary homes. In Harwich, a sizeable town, there was a basic structure of emergency resources and an additional reservoir of able-bodied men like Mr Bentley and Mr Gostling, together with St John Ambulance, W.R.V.S. and Red Cross branches all of whom were able to be mobilised fairly quickly; Jaywick was a straggling community whose

The signpost provides ironic guidance for rescuers at Jaywick on Sunday morning, 1st February.
Press Association

permanent residents were mainly retired folk. The average age of the thirty-seven people who died at Jaywick was sixty-six.

Most of the settlement's 1,800 or so chalets were used only in the summer, but about 250 of them were occupied that night. There is only one way into the place, via Jaywick Lane. By midnight, water was spilling over the sea wall and four policemen were in the area trying to arouse residents and organise relief services. But there was no precise knowledge of which chalets were occupied and which empty, and by that time most people had gone to bed so that there were few lights to show the rescuers where to call. Even for those who were warned, escape was not easy. Most of the chalets had pitched roofs but not all had any means of access. Many people had to smash their way into the roof space through the ceiling. Even then, they were only temporarily and superficially safe; the water was later to lift many chalets off their footings and toss them about like matchboxes. One elderly survivor who managed to climb into her roof space was trapped in darkness with her cat for thirty-one hours after her chalet overturned, with no means of attracting the rescuers' attention. Another lifted a handicapped sister through a window, to feel her snatched away by the torrent outside. A younger man made a dash for it through the front door, with his semi-invalid wife and a three-year-old grandchild. "As we pushed open the door the full force of the water hit us," he said later. "I was up to my neck. My wife just disappeared." He managed to save himself and his grandchild by clinging to a barbed-wire fence until help came.

At nearby Point Clear Bay, the Crosswell family ran a grocery store — a one-storey affair with living quarters at the back — and, on slightly higher ground a few hundred yards away, a cafe. Fifty-eight-year-old William Crosswell and his wife Lilian ran the store and their son Ronald the cafe. When he saw the water rising, Ronald set out down the road to the store to lead his parents out, but when the swirling water reached his thighs he was forced back. There was a tied 'phone line between the two businesses, and Ronald rang his father on this to warn him to get out while he could; there was a two-storey house a few yards from the store where the older Crosswells could have found shelter until the water went down. William Crosswell was still trying to save the goods in the shop by moving them to higher shelves. Ronald again set out to reach his parents, but was again driven back. He telephoned once more. "The windows are coming in," his father reported, and behind him Ronald heard his mother cry out: "Save yourself. We're drowning." They were the last words the older Crosswells ever spoke.

At the Lee-over-Sands holiday estate, only one bungalow was occupied — the manager's. Living there with the manager and his wife were their two grown-up sons and a small daughter, who was ill. They first became aware of trouble when they heard water lapping round the bungalow as they got ready for bed. Looking out, they found that they were completely surrounded, and two of their three boats — the two sons were fishermen — had floated away. Wrapping the sick girl in blankets, they set out for safety in the third boat, with the girl's pony swimming astern. At this time, the water was about five feet deep; it had overtopped the sea wall, but the wall itself was still intact.

The family soon found that their progress was hampered by barbed-wire fences through which they had to cut their way. In doing so, one of the sons fell overboard and became entangled with the wire. As the others struggled to free him, they saw the sea wall breached. The wave that followed lifted them all clear of the wire and carried them inland, snatching four of their six oars out of their hands. It was two hours before they reached dry land, over three miles from their home.

As at other places, there was to be criticism later of the apparent lack of warning for the residents of Jaywick. In fact, according to evidence given at the inquest on the Jaywick victims by Superintendent Arthur Simpson, local police chief at the time, some Jaywick people "thought we were being too alarmist about it all" and ignored the police warnings. Once the flood had struck, its effects were of course beyond the meagre resources of the local police, hampered as they were by the failure of their radio network (the wind had brought down the transmitter masts), the blockage of roads by trees, and the sheer weight of calls on their services. Jaywick's village policeman, Henry Mitchell himself rescued six people before he was joined by colleagues and was eventually marooned for several hours on a bungalow roof. But in spite of individual heroic efforts of this kind, rescue was—initially at any rate, and in some areas for a disturbingly long period of time—a matter of self-help. The elderly, the handicapped and the very young were all at a disadvantage.

There was one last place along the east coast where the tide was to claim victims. This was Canvey Island, another unplanned settlement, at the mouth of the Thames Estuary, where fifty-eight people died. Like so many of the other worst-hit places, Canvey was one of those sprawls of self-built and jerry-built shacks and shanties so typical of the eastern and southern English coastline. Its closeness to London—and especially to east London—made it a popular spot for holiday chalets and retirement homes; under the housing pressures of 1953 many of the properties intended for summer occupation only had been rented or bought for permanent use. The population of Canvey in 1953 was about 10,000, of whom a large proportion, then as now, consisted of commuters to the capital. Also prominent among the people of Canvey were the elderly, many of them fulfilling a lifetime's dream of a home by the sea after retiring from work in London.

Canvey Island was, in a word, overwhelmed quite suddenly, some time after midnight. It was Jaywick all over again, but on a much larger scale. There was no record of which houses were permanently occupied. There was

On an Essex airfield, an R.A.F. bomber stands as helpless as if it had been ditched at sea.
Press Association

Canvey Island on Monday morning, 2nd February. By this time, the decision had been taken to evacuate all the island's population. *Press Association*

then only one road linking Canvey with the mainland, across the bridge leading to Benfleet station. As will be seen in the next chapter, Canvey Island was the scene of the largest single evacuation of the weekend, the entire population eventually being taken off within forty-eight hours, as if from a sinking ship. But there is no concealing that for the few hours of darkness between the time the flood struck and dawn on the Sunday morning — a period of six hours or so — the situation on the island was too confused and too appalling for anyone to handle.

The sea swept over Canvey, indeed, with all the suddenness of a disaster in mid-ocean. A coach party crossing the bridge from Benfleet about midnight had noticed some water lying in Benfleet High Street but, in view of the wildness of the night, considered this not untoward. The members of the outing dispersed to their homes on Canvey, glad to be out of the wind and to get to bed. A few minutes later, at about half past midnight, the island's ordeal began.

Christopher Manser, then thirteen years old, was asleep in the small bungalow in Somner Avenue, hard behind the sea-wall, which he shared with his parents, eight brothers, one sister, and Rufus, the family's fox-terrier. With Rufus at the foot of his bed, and his fifteen-year-old brother Ian beside him, Christopher had settled quickly into a deep sleep. Though very poor, and living in impossibly cramped conditions in a bungalow with only the minimum of amenities—there was gas, but no electricity, and water had to be fetched from a pump at the top of the road—the Manser family was a happy, close-knit one. An added bonus to help Christopher sleep contentedly that night was the thought of the new coat and trousers that his mother had shown him on the Saturday evening. He had always had second-hand clothes before, but tomorrow he would wear new for the first time in his life. The coat and trousers, so carefully saved for, so proudly set out, inspected with such pleasure, were destined never to be worn.

It was about 12.30 a.m. when Christopher was awoken by Rufus's barking. He and Ian got out of bed. "Straightaway," Christopher remembers, "we were up to our waists in ice-cold water. It was pitch dark, and by now the other children were crying out in the other bedrooms." The other children ranged from eleven-year-old Andrew to Geoffrey, eighteen months.

"Somehow," Christopher's story goes on, "we found our parents and gathered in the central room of the bungalow. I was clutching one youngster, Ian another, and my mother had the two babies. The water was rising by the

An eloquent testimony to the desolation of Canvey Island on Sunday morning. For many rescuers, it was a matter of calling and listening for the faint replies. Eye-witnesses at Canvey testify to the eerie sound, that Sunday, of tireless rescuing voices calling across the water.
Press Association

second. My father found his lighter and lit the gas-mantle; it flickered for about four minutes and then went out, but those few minutes gave us a quick look at the situation. Then all was dark again."

The children were all crying and screaming. Some of them had found bits of furniture to stand on, but as the water rose these broke up or floated away. By now, the water was up to Christopher's chest, about four feet six inches deep. He worked out that, as the bungalow was built on stilts two feet six inches high, the depth outside must be at least seven feet.

Behind the bungalow ran the Winter Gardens path, about 500 yards away and raised on a bank. Ian decided to swim to it and raise the alarm. He set off through the barbed-wire, dodging the debris that was now being carried along on the tide. Meanwhile, the rest of the family waited. As their eyes became accustomed to the dark they were just able to pick out each other's positions. Christopher's mother was sitting on a window-sill with the water up to her chest, clutching her two youngest boys, two-year-old Stephen and eighteen-month-old Geoffrey. Christopher himself was trying to keep two other children afloat. His father had the other three.

The cold gnawed at them. Christopher goes on: "I started to get very tired and could not get the children's faces out of the water. We waited for help, but it never came and we thought Ian must have been lost.

My mother made us all shout for help. We found out later that a neighbour in the two-storey house next door had tried to reach us but couldn't make it. The water continued to rise and was now up to my bottom lip. My mother made us shout and sing. We sang hymns. I remember praying to God and promising to go to Sunday School every week if He would only help!"

Then the Mansers thought of a way out that had occurred that night to so many other East Coast families: Christopher's father smashed his fist through the asbestos ceiling, tore away some of the panels, and "standing on the remains of a submerged table, between us we passed up the older children so that they sat straddled across the rafters, out of the water". As Christopher climbed up to join them, the table broke, leaving his mother still sitting on the window-ledge. "We shouted and sang and prayed some more, but no help came."

"The children started to fight and argue. Then one fell in. The water was still rising. I jumped in after him and kept him afloat. There was no means of getting back as all the furniture had gone. I was back where I'd started, and twice as cold and sleepy."

Christopher remembers looking at the peaceful faces of the three youngest children, the one he was supporting and the two still held by his mother. It was only later that he realised that their peace was the peace of death.

Logically, the next place in the line of the surge should have been London, and in fact there was a good deal of damage to industrial installations along the banks of the Thames Estuary. The river level even in central London rose to an alarming height, lapping at the top of the parapets on the Victoria and Chelsea embankments. But in the early hours of Sunday morning the wind backed, and the surge swung away across the North Sea towards Holland. Here, according to an official account, "more than fifty dykes burst almost simultaneously and nearly half a million acres of polder* country were swallowed by the raging sea. Nearly 1,800 people are known to have been drowned, over 50,000 evacuated, about 50,000 cattle and 100,000 hens lost." Shattering as the night had been for the people of eastern England, for the Dutch is was much worse, flooding about nine per cent of the country's agricultural land and destroying over 1,000 farms.

Nonetheless, while most of Britain slept peacefully, thousands of her people lived through the first hours of Sunday, 1st February, 1953 in a state of bewilderment, like the old people rescued from Snettisham Beach in Norfolk; or abject terror, like the Ridleys of Sea Palling; or teetering between life and death, like the Mansers of Canvey Island. For all of them, life would never be the same again. And for some 300 more, life was over.

*Land reclaimed from the sea.

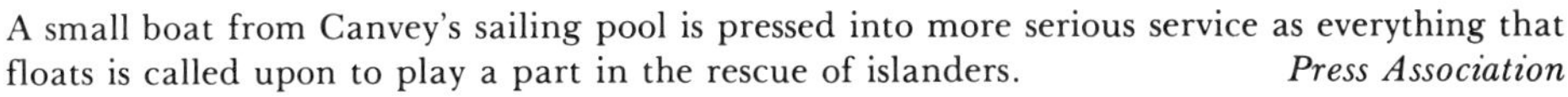

A small boat from Canvey's sailing pool is pressed into more serious service as everything that floats is called upon to play a part in the rescue of islanders. *Press Association*

CHAPTER FOUR

WHEN the dawn came on Sunday, the east coast of England was an appalling sight; just how appalling could be appreciated only by the R.A.F. crews who were sent out at first light to take aerial photographs of the devastation in "Operation Floodlight", which was to continue for several days. The monstrous surge in the night had made nonsense of the maps. Along three-quarters of the coastline, the defences had been damaged, and huge lengths—like the thirty-four miles from Cleethorpes to Skegness—almost completely destroyed. South of Mablethorpe and Sutton-on-Sea, some 22,000 acres of prime agricultural land lay under the sea water that poured in through a gap in the sea-wall one-third of a mile long, the biggest of the many breaches. The bank between Kings Lynn and Hunstanton, with its formerly neat line of beach-huts and bungalows, had been reduced to a shambles of driftwood, with caravans and shanties lying on their sides in the water like toys. The north Norfolk villages of Salthouse and Cley, normally well inland, had become waterside settlements which looked as if they had been blitzed. The cliffs of north-east Norfolk showed several new shallow bays that the sea had carved out during the night. Great Yarmouth and its hinterland were unrecognisable from the air. Further south, Foulness and Canvey had become half-submerged offshore islands, with many of their residents still a day or more from rescue. The surge had driven up the Thames Estuary and taken over large stretches of industrial land close to the river. Pressing on, it had made incursions round the Kent coast as far as Deal.

The tallies of damage were added up later: over 300 lives had been lost, over 24,000 houses damaged, 200 industrial premises flooded and put out of action, along with twelve gasworks and two power stations, eleven trunk roads made impassable, 200 miles of railway track out of use, 160,000 acres of agricultural land rendered sterile for a season at least and in many cases for years, 9,000 sheep lost, 1,100 head of cattle, 2,600 pigs, 34,000 head of poultry, 70 horses . . . Perhaps it was fortunate for morale that the statistics were not available that Sunday morning. For those in the affected areas, the devastation and suffering immediately facing them was enough to cope with.

Along the coast bordering the Wash, where the surge had struck early, and indeed the next tide had come and gone before daybreak, it was a Sunday morning for counting the cost and sorting out the mess. There was even time for residents to reflect on the horror they had been through. Further south, in the virtually submerged coastal settlements of Essex, there was still urgent

Scenes like this, brought back by the R.A.F. and aircraft chartered by the Press, led Essex rescue workers to fear the worst for the 400 or so residents of Foulness Island. These pictures were taken on Monday, 2nd February, some 40 hours after the flood struck. It was about the same time that Southend lifeboat reported having made contact with people who had taken shelter on the top floors of their homes. *Press Association*

rescue work to be done. At this stage, however, every area was still more or less dependent upon its own resources: local police and firemen, ambulance crews both full-time and voluntary, the Women's Voluntary Service and other remnants of wartime Civil Defence which still existed haphazardly, and of course the many people with no occupational or organisational commitments who turned up to see what needed to be done.

Daybreak found the stricken Manser family of Canvey Island near to exhaustion—and still without help. Eventually, a kayak turned up, and the two men in it began to ferry the children one by one to the Winter Garden bank. By the time it was Christopher's turn, he had been in the water for ten and a half hours. "I was carried frozen stiff and going to sleep," he remembers, "to a house on a high piece of ground, just off the Winter Garden wall. A woman put me in blankets, hot water bottles all round, and rubbed and rubbed until I came round. How I blessed her!"

The house by the wall was only temporary sanctuary, however. Another tide was due. Given dry, warm clothing that, he says, was ten times too big for him, Christopher Manser was sent to walk along the wall to Benfleet. "As I got

466

to the cottages near the station an old lady took me in and gave me a cup of cocoa." When he was united with his family at the rest centre he found that his elder brother Ian, who had swum out into the night to find help, had survived but the three youngest children, ranging in age from three years to eighteen months, had died of exposure.

Among the early visitors to Canvey that Sunday morning was Martin Lyon, then living in London, whose parents-in-law lived on the Island. Reaching the level crossing at Benfleet—Canvey's Checkpoint Charlie—he was turned back by a police guard as he had not means of identification justifying his going on. He was directed to an emergency information centre where lists of the rescued were pinned up; his in-laws' names were not among them, and neither did they appear on the notice-boards at the other information centres to which Mr Lyon was directed. He returned to the crossing-point and began to plead for permission to go on to Canvey. "Luck came at that moment," he remembers. "A local taxi pulled up and the occupant happened to be a person known to me. She vouched for me, and agreed to share the taxi on to the Island."

The taxi took Mr Lyon as far as the Red Cow pub (now, with grisly humour, re-named the "King Canute"). This was at the edge of the flood water, which was about ankle-deep at that time. "I rolled up my trouser-legs," Mr Lyon recalls, "and continued my unpleasant journey. The water was getting deeper and I felt defeated. It was a couple of minutes after I felt in an impossible position—marooned, cold, hungry, depressed—that I heard in the distance what sounded like loud voices. I strained my ears and listened.

At this stage the scene was extremely eerie: dead silence except for the ripples of the water caused by the cold breeze. The flotsam was profuse and varied; it included chickens, goats, cats, toilet pails and buckets—anything that was unattached and able to float was floating."

The voices turned out to be those of a party of St John Ambulance men in a large rowing-boat with a dinghy attached, shouting in turn: "Anybody about? Anybody about?" They took Mr Lyon aboard, lent him a towel to dry himself with and gave him a drink of tea from their flask. When he explained his mission, they lent him the dinghy and oars, warning him that he would need to bale out quite a bit as the dinghy was taking in a lot of water.

"Away I rowed with renewed energy," Mr Lyon's story goes on. "Fortunately I could set my course as the crow flies directly to my goal; I rowed a bit and baled a bit. At one point I thought my journey was over; my dinghy got hooked on a gutter section of a bungalow. But after a struggle I got it free, and eventually reached my in-laws' bungalow.

Luckily the land was rather higher at this point, and on inspection from the top window I could see that they had systematically packed up and gone, leaving goods and chattels stacked as near ceiling-height as possible."

Strict control was kept on visitors to Canvey after the flood. Only those with legitimate business were allowed through. Here, at the bridge which was Canvey's only link with the mainland, the police check new arrivals from the train. *Press Association*

There were over 40 breaks in the sea defences at Canvey Island alone, and with a fortnight to go before the spring tides it was essential to move fast. By Tuesday, 3rd February, bundles of sandbags were being delivered by lorry and in some places by air, while National Servicemen from all over southern and eastern England were rushed to the scene to fill the bags and place them in position. Apart from their sterling work on the defences, the involvement of the servicemen helped to spread news of the intensity of the flood disaster throughout the country, and this was reflected in the public's response. Some servicemen are shown here working near the Red Cow, Canvey. *Press Association*

Comforted by the assumption that his relatives were safe, he rowed back the way he had come; "the only other person I encountered was a Salvation Army officer in a small boat seeking anybody who needed help in any way". After the long journey back, he 'phoned home to London to discover that in the meantime his parents-in-law had rung to say that they were safe: "Had they 'phoned in the first place," Mr Lyon comments, "letting us know all was well, I would not have had that nightmare experience."

Meanwhile, at Cley on the north Norfolk coast, H. H. Rich went round his property to assess the damage. This is what he found:

"To take it in bits. A foot to eighteen inches of small bits of reed over the whole of the ground floor. We couldn't open any door, they were jammed with it. Both front doors were down, and the outer one has gone . . . The inner one and most of the lintel was inside the house. The bottom glass of the kitchen and hall windows smashed. The whole window-frame of the dining-room driven inwards."

It was a feature of the sudden impact of water and wind that its effects were curiously selective and irrational; those who have experienced bomb-blast have reported a similar phenomenon. Mr Rich's morning-after report went on:

"Now for the rooms. Don't forget the bed of reeds everywhere.

Kitchen. Fridge overturned, Calor gas cylinders overturned, but no escape of gas and it has worked since it dried out. Everything else below the level of the sink a shambles. Very little broken, I think because of the reeds.

Hall. Table well down the passage.

Dining-room. Both chests of drawers overturned. The table pushed against the wall. Chairs everywhere. The glass cupboard with plates and glasses intact and very little broken.

Sitting-room. Chests of drawers overturned. Plenty of mud and things unmoved as you approached the window . . .

From the water marks we had between two and three feet of water inside the house.

Outside. The front wall nearly flat. The wall between the front and the vegetable garden the same . . . The big wooden shed had bodily floated intact and was only stopped as it reached the house . . . The carpenter's shop split and open to the sky . . . Outside the drawing-room window is a mass of reeds, rabbit-hutches and goodness knows what. I nearly forgot, there was a boat nestling outside the dining-room window."

The boat, incidentally, was still in the garden when the carpenter arrived some weeks later to start making the front of Mr Rich's house weatherproof.

"That's my boat," cried the carpenter. It had been washed away from Blakeney, two miles distant.

Heartbreaking though it must have been to set about trying to restore life to normal—faced with chaos like this, the Rich family (and indeed Cley itself, with only one death) were comparatively lucky. Over at Snettisham Beach, H. W. Temple Cole was dazed by what the morning revealed:

"The front of the beach is cleared of all the timber sea wall and only about twenty bungalows are left in ruins, out of over one hundred. Some of these were removed bodily under the line of overhead electric cable, across the big pitholes dug out for the shingle works, across the shunting yards where they keep the shingle trucks, over a high hedge, over a line of bungalows at a lower level, and finally landed on top of the flood bank, at least eight or nine hundred yards from the original site, and still remained more or less whole, with most of the china intact inside. Others were completely smashed to firewood and not a sign of them is left. The bungalows at the back suffered a similar fate, and I do not think that there are more than half a dozen left habitable anywhere between the village and the sea. Some of the debris travelled well over a mile and a half from its original position."

Sixty-one lives had been lost along the short stretch of coast between Hunstanton and Lynn, most of them at Snettisham, Heacham and Hunstanton

South Beach, though this total was not appreciated until several days later. The toll included several complete American service families living near Hunstanton.

Wells butcher and farmer Charles Ramm was up early and down on the marshes to see what the damage was. His pasture land was unrecognisable. Just how forcefully the water had swept across it was demonstrated by the haystack that had been lifted from the field in one piece and left stranded, without a bale out of place, on top of one of the inner banks. At Holkham station, the railway embankment had been washed away and the line from Burnham Market to Wells curved away into the water. It was never to reopen.

"There were dead cattle everywhere," Mr Ramm remembers. He had lost fifteen of his seventy-five store cattle, but the fate of his flock of sheep was much worse: there were only thirteen survivors out of 215. Even if sheep had an instinct for survival to call upon, they could not obey it: the weight of their sodden wool pulls them down. Mr Ramm found fifteen of his cattle, however, marooned on two of the wartime pill-boxes that littered the area. They were rescued later when boatmen from Wells, on their way to rescue a stranded couple at Meals House, near the sea bank, frightened the cattle into swimming for it. "Much to my surprise," Mr Ramm says, "they swam more than a hundred yards. I'd never seen anything like it before or since." Another beast, a Devon bullock, had scrambled up on to the platform at Holkham station. It was not until the Tuesday afternoon, nearly three days later, that it could be rescued. In the meantime, Mr Ramm took it fresh water by boat. One of his other beasts had been drinking salt water, and it had "turned him funny in the head, though he got over it eventually". Meanwhile, there was the problem of finding fresh pasture for the survivors. The sea was to pour in through the breach at Wells for seven weeks, covering the fields twice a day, and even on higher ground there was salt water in the dykes. The problem was solved for Mr Ramm with the loan of a meadow in Holkham Park from his landlord, Lord Leicester.

Among livestock, sheep—their fleeces holding the water and dragging them down—were the most vulnerable to flood water. Collecting their carcases was one of the disagreeable tasks that had to be done as the water receded. The scene here is just outside Wells. The railway line in the background, from Hunstanton and Burnham Market, was irreparably damaged by flood water and was never to re-open. *Walmsley and Webb*

At this stage, the inhabitants of many isolated villages up and down the coast thought, like those of Holkham, that they had been the victims of a purely local disaster. "We thought we were the only ones," one farmer's wife remembers. It was only when Lord Leicester and his agent had climbed Holkham church tower and reported back to the tenants that they realised that the sea was all around.

From Model Farm, Holkham, Mr and Mrs Harris Wroth went down to the marshes to see what had happened. It was devastating, Mrs Wroth remembers, to look at the height of the tide-line and what had been washed up there: sheep by the score, wildfowl suddenly overwhelmed by the surge and unable to rise in the wind, pheasants caught in the trees. And still, the wind. The wind went on throughout Sunday, and remains Mrs Wroth's outstanding memory of the floods: "You couldn't hear yourself speak, you could hardly stand against it. I kept thinking, if only that wind would drop." For the Wroths' neighbour, Mary Hancock, the memory of the "tangle" — the tide-line of animal and vegetable debris — still raised a shudder twenty-three years later.

Along the coast at Sea Palling, the debris of the morning after was even more grim. Farmer's wife Kathleen Deary remembers that "the farm fields were strewn with furniture, including chests of drawers full of linen and able to be returned to the owners". But others in Sea Palling were less fortunate: "Mr and Mrs Holmes, who owned the shop and bakery, walked out when the water began to come in. They went back next morning and had lost everything. There wasn't a brick left from the house and shop." Florence Ridley, also of Sea Palling, remembers "the sense of loss on looking at the desolation, not only of our home but of the whole village".

Just north of Sea Palling, H. Grantham-Hill spent Sunday morning "moving the possessions of a Mrs Challoner to safety; she was an ancient lady living alone in a house which was partly over the cliff edge". Later in the day, he went to Walcott Post Office Stores, "whose front door now opened immediately on to the cliff and made the posting of a letter a perilous procedure", and helped out there.

If one of the peculiarities of the disaster was that "we thought we were the only ones", another was that most people who were not immediately involved, even in an adjacent street or a couple of hundred yards up a lane, knew little except that it had been a rough night. At Southwold, in Suffolk, for example, Joan Priday and a friend took the dog for a walk at about 9.30 p.m. on Saturday evening, about half an hour before the surge reached the small seaside town. The wind, Miss Priday remembers, was strong — "it was as much as you could do to stand" — but they went home and slept peacefully nonetheless. Next morning, between 9 and 10 a.m., they took the dog out again — "our usual walk to the common, where we were suddenly confronted by the ocean. The common had just vanished — it was sea right to the horizon".

The early visit to flooded areas by Her Majesty the Queen and the Duke of Edinburgh was more than a mere official token of interest. Sandringham is only four miles from the stricken stretch of coastline between Kings Lynn and Hunstanton. Here, Her Majesty visits Snettisham beach. Later, she went on to talk to survivors at a Kings Lynn rest centre.

This was their first intimation of anything amiss. At Felixstowe, Councillor B. Haste was later to complain about the delay in engaging local helpers. "I am vexed to know that I did not know the extent of damage before ten o'clock on Sunday morning," he told an emergency meeting of Felixstowe Council on the Wednesday after the flood. "I am certain others feel as I do, that had we known, there would have been a greater response from us earlier in the day."

Possibly, if the day had been any other than a Sunday news might have travelled faster as people got up and about and went to work. As it was, with telephones along the coastal strip largely out of action, and given the general somnolence of provincial England on a Sunday morning in winter, news of the floods spread slowly. This was as true nationally as locally. The big story in the Sunday papers was still the loss of the *Princess Victoria* off Scotland, and brief news of the floods made only the late editions, which did not go to the east coast. The B.B.C.'s morning news bulletins mentioned the floods, but concentrated mainly on the *Princess Victoria* story. Today, when news is so highly organised that press, radio and television would have been on to the story within hours, if not minutes, it seems incredible that a large part of the country was to remain in ignorance of the 1953 disaster until Monday, but it was so; and even then, *The Times*, for example, dismissed the events of the weekend in 600 words. Sara Sproule of Burnham Norton, then staying in London, remembers how slowly information came through: "It was extraordinary how long it took before you could believe what had happened, even though you had a place there. As soon as the Queen came down there, then pictures began to hit the press, and you began to think about it then. Our tenants rang up and said, 'We've had the floods in,' but you *still* didn't have any information until you went down and saw where the water had been, and thought, 'If I'd been standing here, it would have been thirty feet above me'."

As far as local government was concerned, the main east coast administrative centres of Lincoln, Norwich, Chelmsford and Ipswich were themselves unaffected by flooding, and by the time the harrassed emergency services on the ground could find time from their life-saving and other urgent duties to alert the county offices the day was well advanced. Some volunteers had heard the news and turned up at their offices to offer their help; but there was no recognised call-out system such as exists today. Contact with national sources of help proved even more difficult; at 2.30 p.m. on Sunday afternoon a desperate Essex County Council official trying to get hold of an emergency supply of blankets for the rest centres rang the Ministry of Housing and Local Government in London—to receive no reply.

The consequence of all this was that help from outside seemed to come agonisingly slowly for local organisations and local people who had in many cases been working flat out all night. This was to give rise later to bitter criticism that the people of the east coast had been doubly let down: first by the failure to warn them that flooding was likely, and second by the delay before relief arrived.

The criticism was perhaps unfair—though it might have been reasonable to expect the Ministry of Housing and Local Government, for example, to make an earlier start—if only because of the number of different dimensions in which help was urgently needed. Provision for rescued and evacuated families, many of them with only the night-clothes they were wearing when the flood struck, was the first priority, closely followed by the need to carry out emergency repairs to the worst of the breaches in the defences. Emergency food supplies, communications, fuel stocks and water had also to be arranged. Gas and electricity services, water supplies, sewage disposal and, of course, normal drainage had all been interrupted. To take just one example of the havoc the night had brought: in the Eastern Electricity Board's area, covering Norfolk, Suffolk and Essex, over 47,500 homes lost their electricity supplies.

Within forty-eight hours, nearly two-thirds of these had had their supply restored. Further ahead lay the problems of surveying and restoring damaged property, pumping out trapped water from between internal flood banks, disposing of the dead farm animals and sorting out the survivors. For unlike disasters of the man-made world—rail or air crashes, pit accidents, shipping losses—natural disasters are followed inevitably by a long haul back to normality. There was hardly any aspect of life round the east coast, from the Post Office's problems in trying to deliver mail correctly to thousands of evacuated families to the sheer economic survival of hundreds of farmers, that was not affected for months (and in some cases years) to come by the events of Saturday, 31st January. Worries varied in scale from those of Essex County Council officials, who needed 35,000 blankets by Sunday night for evacuees, to those of individual pensioners who, in the rush to get away from their flooded homes, had left their pension and ration books behind.

Few records exist of the unexpected and hastily-convened Sunday meetings of local councils and other organisations along the coastal strip, because everyone who attended was more concerned with action than with taking minutes. The early records of the Great Yarmouth Flood Relief Committee, formed that Sunday morning, consist, typically, of pencilled notes about blankets and sandbags, some names and addresses of local contacts, and some hasty calculations in the margin. But already the next tide was sweeping down the coast, three-quarters of which lay breached and tattered and exposed. In Lichfield Road, Great Yarmouth, Jack Loveday was relieved to find, at breakfast-time on Sunday, that the water that had driven his family upstairs

On the Sunday, residents of Burnham Overy Town wade through the water left behind when the sea receded. "Topped up" at each high tide through the breach in Overy Staithe Bank, flood water remained on the land in this area for weeks. Behind the hedge between the houses, the sea floods what was formerly (and is now again) good pasture; but it was several years before farming returned to normal in north-west Norfolk. *Gilbert White*

overnight had retreated, though it had left in its wake "a dreadful layer of filth and a tide-mark round the walls". But his relief was short-lived, for by mid-morning the water was returning, this time through the back door. "Luckily," Mr Loveday remembers, "the gas stayed on and by wading through waist-deep water I was able to reach the gas stove in the kitchen, boil a kettle and give the baby her feed. Though marooned upstairs, we took no harm."

Indeed, according to Mr Loveday's account, as the day wore on there was a kind of post-disaster euphoria in the air, similar to the chirpiness shown by London people emerging from Tube shelters after the Blitz. "The sun shone on the water flowing along the street," Mr Loveday recalls, "and with people shouting to each other from bedroom windows there was a kind of wartime excitement about it. Floating by we could see timber, apples, carrots and on one occasion a settee."

But the cheerfulness was short-lived: "At sunset we were less buoyant when the water, which we had expected to disappear, did not go down. Darkness made things seem depressing, so at 6.30 p.m. we heard that our friends along the road were leaving in a rescue lorry and decided to do likewise. Eventually, I waded out to a lorry, my wife and baby being carried out, together with the lady from whom we rented the rooms.

The lorry took us to the Town Hall, a very cold ride on an open vehicle. The passengers' ages ranged from Anita, our baby of five months, to a lady of ninety who sat huddled in a corner of the lorry clutching a small lamp."

In Felixstowe, a surprised resident in the Langer Road area ventured downstairs when the water had retreated to find two pigs in his front room, sitting at either end of the settee. In Landguard Road, an elderly man rigged up a clothes-line in front of a bedroom fire and pegged up his life's savings, in one-pound notes, to dry. In Wells, Norfolk, people gathered to marvel at the 160-ton torpedo boat which had been lifted clean out of the harbour by the surge and deposited high and dry on the quay. (The boat stayed there until September, when the people of Wells gathered again to see it returned to the water, perhaps as a symbol that the disaster was behind them.)

As the short February day went on, however, the position of marooned families along some of the more isolated and shattered parts of the Essex coast became increasingly desperate. Probably the most dramatic events of the day took place at Canvey Island, where by using every available means of transport—coaches, buses, taxis, private cars and boats—some 10,000 people had been evacuated by midnight on Sunday, leaving about 1,000 still on the island, of whom about half were evacuated the next day. But further north at Foulness, the 400 or so residents, cut off by a five-mile stretch of rough water, could not be reached until Monday. At one stage it was feared, after a reconnaissance flight had reported no sign of life on the island, that all must have been drowned, but a later flight just before dusk confirmed that there

Canvey Island, Monday 2nd February. The great evacuation has begun, and buses take unscheduled routes. *Press Association*

were people still alive in upstairs rooms. There was, of course, no other means of contact with the islanders, and while preparations were made for a dawn landing by boats, volunteers and officials on the mainland prepared for the worst, which may well have included, for all they knew, several hundred dead. Monday's dawn landing was effected by a Dunkirk-style flotilla of "little ships" ranging from a Thames barge through oyster boats to the Southend lifeboat, and all but two of the islanders were still alive. The only contact Foulness people had had with the outside world for some thirty hours was a B.B.C. message broadcast to them at Sunday midnight promising them rescue in the morning.

By Sunday night some 40,000 people from the east coast were sheltering in makeshift rest centres: schools (including one in Essex whose head teacher had been reluctant to open up in case the new paint was damaged), church halls, village halls, social clubs, holiday camps, pubs, hotels, boarding-houses, service camps, factory hostels. The evacuees were sustained at this stage by local effort—soup from the Salvation Army, tea and sandwiches from the Women's Voluntary Services, medical aid from local doctors, district nurses and the St John Ambulance Brigade, beds and bedding from the Red Cross, and such services as sending telegrams to relatives from local people who had just "dropped in" to see what needed to be done. The Salvation Army, the St John Ambulance Brigade, "R.A.F. and U.S.A.F. boys" who turned up with huge drying-machines, and individual householders who ran do-it-yourself refreshments for the rescue and relief workers figure prominently in the grateful memories of my correspondents and contacts. As early as one o'clock on Sunday morning, Clifford Eaton, owner of Felixstowe's Cavendish Hotel, had opened up the ballroom as a reception centre. One of those who called by later on Sunday was Ipswich schoolmaster Edward Sillett, who soon found himself taking over the organisation of the place. Incoming and outgoing flood victims were registered, a fleet of cars organised to pass them on to more official rest centres, and food and emergency clothes arranged. Mr Sillett was to stay at the hotel for two weeks.

It must be said here that the promptness with which voluntary organisations—whom one might have thought least well-equipped to deal with a disaster of such devastating proportions and suddenness—reacted was in sharp contrast to the sloth of officialdom further afield. That government shut down so firmly at weekends was something of a revelation to people who had never had to consider the matter before. With some shining exceptions, including the armed forces, it was not however until Monday that the government machine began to stir itself to action.

The immediate problems of caring for the homeless and setting about the task of repairing damaged homes were bad enough; but, looking further ahead, the prospect that faced the east coast was that in a fortnight's time the next spring tides were due, predicted to be two feet higher than those of 31st January. In many places, the authorities, within the time available, could do little more than watch and pray that the new moon springs would at least not widen the breaches. One week after the flood, all but about 150 acres of the 4,000 acres of agricultural land inundated in the East Riding of Yorkshire had been cleared, but the East Riding had got off comparatively lightly: "the force of the flood water," an official report noted, "was insufficient to scour the land nearby." By contrast, the 2,000 or so acres of the Holkham estate in north Norfolk, about eight per cent of the Leicester land, which had been flooded were to remain under tidal water for several months.

Early on the morning of 2nd February, river board engineers were out on the melancholy job of assessing the damage to the sea defences, the reasons for failure, and the need for immediate action. Their notes make sober reading. The Lincolnshire River Board's officers, for example, found that at South Killingholme Haven, "two separate soils involved in the construction of the bank . . . were not bonded together and a plane of weakness between them . . . contributed to the collapse of the knife-edge crest". At Woodfarm Bank, near Grimsby, they reported that "lump chalk deposited by barges each year (was) too soft for this kind of work and too readily broke up into small pebbles and was washed away". At Mablethorpe, "stepped concrete walls broke up. Paving slabs and road kerbs were ripped out and carried into town together with sand and mud". At Sutton-on-Sea, "three to four feet of sand reaches up to the window-sills of the bungalows, and the road is level with the sills". As noted in Chapter One, the river boards had only recently taken over responsibility for sea defences; this first detailed survey of their manors, undertaken under pressure, was to reveal how patchy had been the maintenance and construction of the banks under the old regime.

The major weapon in the fight to build up a temporary barrage before the night of 13th-14th February was one which was, mercifully, so soon after the Second World War, still in good supply: the sandbag. Many men doing their National Service in 1953 remember what was for them a hard-working but nevertheless welcome break in routine when they were sent to the east coast to help in the great sandbag war. They were joined by almost every building worker available — and in Essex alone some 4,000 farmers and their men volunteered to join in. Literally millions of sandbags arrived by road and rail, to be filled by the waiting task-force. In most places, plenty of sand was available for the digging in the saltings, but the availability of men and materials did not solve all the problems. A later report by the East Suffolk and Norfolk River Board, then responsible for the sea-defences between Hunstanton and Felixstowe, explained: "The greatest problem of all the emergency works was access, because few cross-walls exist in the Board's area and practically all the frontal walls were breached, and therefore only methods of repair based on self-contained labour units were successful. This explains the vast requirements of civil and military labour that were necessary in the early stages of the work . . . In certain instances, landing barges were employed to dump slag directly into large breaches, but this was both a hazardous and uncertain procedure and, in general, was not entirely successful . . . In the case of a clay wall that failed near Yarmouth, access conditions were particularly difficult and the earliest repair works were carried out by rowing sand-filled bags out over the marshes to the breaches in many scores of small boats."

One of the most serious breaches — though light in terms of casualties — was at Magdalen, south of Kings Lynn, where the surge funnelled up the Great Ouse and broke through the river bank. Thousands of acres were flooded at Watlington, Stow, Magdalen, Salters Lode and St Germans, and the area became the focus of a desperate effort to plug the breach.

Walmsley and Webb

At Magdalen, sandbags were filled on the spot and loaded into barges and a Dunkirk-style flotilla of little boats, to be taken out to the gap. There was exactly a fortnight before the next high tides were due. In that time, the breach must be filled, at least temporarily. Civilian labour—fortunately plentiful in midwinter—was recruited from all over Britain to join National Servicemen and Cambridge students in the task. *Walmsley and Webb*

As the first week of February wore on, the fight to fill the gaps slipped into top gear. By mid-week, contractors were at work on the Lincolnshire coast, and a steady flow of bulldozers, draglines, low-loaders, pumps and other plant built up in East Anglia, followed by engineers from other river boards unaffected by the floods and more civilian and military labour. Searchlights were rigged up so that work could go on round the clock, and by 7th February the East Suffolk and Norfolk River Board had at its disposal about 3,500 servicemen, nearly 1,000 civilian labourers, fifty bulldozers, forty draglines and a selection of twenty-three large pumps.

Meanwhile, any spare labour was being recruited by local building firms, who were coping with an unforeseen rush of business at what is normally the quietest time of the year. Some indication of what all this meant to one comparatively modest firm is given by H. W. Temple Cole of Snettisham, in an account written a few days after the floods: "Our firm have once again been called in for all manner of jobs; firstly to supply men and lorries to help in rescue work at Hunstanton; then to provide trestles and planks for the mortuaries: lending men and portable electric tools to the undertaker so that he could keep pace with the sudden rush of work; providing lorries for ten days to cart water to houses in Hunstanton, as the sea-water got into the waterworks and could not be cleared for quite a while. We then rushed sandbags from central dumps to emergency repairs. Finally, we were called in

"Operation Sandbag" under way. An R.A.F. Hastings from West Malling in Kent makes a drop over Sheppey. 8,000 sandbags could be carried at a time. *Press Association*

to repair several places in the sea-wall at Hunstanton, as there were seven major breaches and about as many minor ones, with a considerable amount of scouring behind, and a large amount of damage to the bathing pool and boating lake. We have several gangs on this work with bulldozers, draglines, compressors and concrete mixers with the usual smaller trimmings, in addition to our normal jobs. We are confident that all the major points of damage will be sealed off before the high tides are due in a few days' time . . ."

Mr Temple Cole's confidence was justified. The local River Board was able to report later that the tides of 13th-14th February passed off without mishap, though there were still several large breaches to be filled at Wells, Breydon, Aldeburgh and Bawdsey.

J. L. B. Crane of Dereham was one of those who volunteered for work on the coast, travelling by coach to the north Norfolk village of Cley, whose protective shingle bank had given way. "Our job," Mr Crane remembers, "was to clear the debris from houses, gardens and farms. The receding water had left a thick layer of mud with quantities of dead and decaying animals and fish. The inhabitants had found the task of cleaning up beyond them. They had managed to clear a few houses and individual rooms in others, but it was a struggle for them to keep going. The danger to health was becoming imminent.

We were amazed to find that the deposit of decaying debris extended on to relatively high ground which one would have expected to be well clear of the surge of water. Inland of the village a boat lay at the top of a sloping field—I remember seeing it still there months afterwards."

Even those farmers who had not lost their livestock and whose land had not been submerged had their problems. Mr Crane helped to clear one farm where the milking sheds were damaged and full of debris and the milking machines out of action. "It was a full-time job for the farmer and his employees to keep the cows fed and milked by hand. They had no time to start restoring the farm to order."

But life had to go on. Kathleen Deary of Sea Palling remembers that she and her husband looked after an aunt and uncle for several nights after the flood. "The aunt, still so keen to make her own butter, made it in my kitchen, which believe me was also afloat by the time she had finished with the pails of water."

It was Kathleen Deary's husband, Herbert, who with another villager had saved Florence Ridley's father when he fell exhausted into a boat. What happened to the Ridley family after the rescue described in Chapter Two was typical of thousands of east coast families in the weeks following the flood. They were taken first to the local pub, which had been set up as a first aid centre, to be given spirits, hot water bottles and tea; and then to a holiday camp at Hemsby, where they were to stay in a chalet for a day or two. "We were told to try to get some rest and to keep warm," Florence Ridley remembers, "but all we could do was cry, all four of us. We really broke down." The wind was still strong. When Florence went across to collect early-morning tea, "the lady laid up a tray for me, but as I stepped out the whole thing was blown out of my hands and the last I saw of it was the things bowling towards Yarmouth". After Hemsby, the family was moved to a country club at Sutton, where they stayed for eight weeks. "Finally we were allowed to go to Palling to see our home. The state of our home—well, the bungalow had shifted sixteen inches on its foundations. The furniture and anything moveable had been swept away. The floor was inches thick in wet sand. Everywhere was desolation. I felt hopelessly lost. I just did not know what to do or how to act."

In fact, the Ridleys' bungalow at Palling was finished, and they moved to Stalham, about four miles away. But their lives, too, had been shattered, like those of many others on the east coast. Florence Ridley says: "My own parents never really got over the shock of that awful night. I myself still remember it and re-live it whenever we have a heavy storm. People tell me I am silly and that I should forget; but how can I sweep from my mind that awful huge wave that engulfed our home and swept the moveable things away? That terrifying struggle up to the village out of the nightmare weather into warmth and among people again? That fearful feeling of water right through to the skin and dripping down, leaving the sand to chafe the skin for days after? The sense of loss of looking at the desolation? The desperate struggle to get my parents and Eva back to health and the heartbreaking effort to dig out some of our home, most of it lost for ever? Then the long, long toil of building up another home . . . Still the memories flood back of that bungalow under the hills, close to the sea we loved, the hopes there that we would live our lives in quiet and peace . . ."

Jack Loveday, too, was sobered when, tired of travelling daily to and from his in-laws' house in north Norfolk, he decided to return on his own to his rooms in Great Yarmouth. He had been back earlier, to find the doors warped, the wallpaper hanging in sheets, and the place smelling like a sewer; but when he heard at the end of February that some of the neighbours had moved back he decided to follow them and start setting the place to rights. In the event he stood it for only one night. The health authorities were still discouraging the return of evacuees until the water supplies had been cleared and houses declared free of contamination by sewage, and one of the means employed was to keep the electricity supply cut off. Jack Loveday "found the damp house with its ill-fitting, creaking doors rather eerie by candlelight!" It was another three weeks before, with the electricity restored, the Loveday family moved back. Among the gifts they received, Jack especially remembers the bottle of wine from Samos with which they were able to celebrate their return.

Sunday morning at Harwich, where, as elsewhere in East Anglia, St John Ambulance and Salvation Army volunteers were well to the fore in rescue and relief work.
East Anglian Daily Times

There were no celebrations, and no return, however, for the Mansers of Canvey Island. The loss of the three youngest children, and of their home, broke the family's spirit. Christopher, then thirteen, remembers his particular grief over the loss of "photographs and personal things, bits of family history that could never be replaced". Something else that was irreplaceable was Christopher's loss of schooling during the period of re-settlement into a new home in Southend: "later when I did go to regular school I could not concentrate and never caught up." For several nights after the flood, the Mansers slept on top of tables and desks at a rest centre. Something that stands out in Christopher's memory of this period is the warmth generated by the spontaneous reaction of local people to the need for clothes: "It was easy," he remembers, "to see how quickly they had reacted to the disaster. Women had taken their husbands' jackets and trousers straight from the wardrobe without even emptying pockets. I found money, cigarettes, diaries and so on." There were also letters and gifts from Yorkshire, Surrey, Canada and Australia, and "we constantly received invitations from families to stay". Local Round Tablers and Rotarians sponsored a trip for the older children to an ice show at Olympia; "I was so grateful for anything that would take our minds off our loss".

For the Mansers, life, which had never been easy, remained infinitely worse. After two temporary moves, they were offered a rented house in Southend and "we were given second-hand furniture, army beds and a few bits and pieces. I suppose my father was given some money, but I never knew how much". But "my father never worked properly again due to ill-health. We were never again 'one big happy family'. I was angry at what life had done to the family, and nobody was the same any more."

As Jack Loveday noted, there was a certain elemental eerieness about houses abandoned during the floods, akin perhaps to that of blitzed houses during the war. Passers-by could get a unique insight into family lives caught, as it were, with their pants down. In some cases literally torn from their beds, families had no time to set their affairs in order. It was so for Mrs Crawford,* who lived in one of the houses in Bathside, Harwich, which had been abandoned. She and her husband, with their son, found temporary refuge with a widow in Dovercourt, who noticed that "Mrs Crawford seemed very nervous, constantly drumming her fingers on the table". Her nervousness increased when her husband was taken to hospital with suspected typhoid. Then, one Saturday, Mrs Crawford herself disappeared.

The mystified neighbours had only to wait for the Sunday papers to find the cause of Mrs Crawford's unease: "There, on the front page, was a report," a then teenage neighbour remembers. "When the electricians had gone into the lofts of the Bathside houses to rewire they had discovered at Mrs Crawford's house, a suitcase containing several tiny baby skeletons."

Mr Crawford, in his hospital bed, also read the report. "If only she had told me," he said, "I'd have put the suitcase out of the window." In the circumstances following the flood, no one, of course, could have traced it. But Mrs Crawford was eventually caught and sentenced to two years in prison, maintaining to the last that her children, with the exception of the one survivor, had all been stillborn—a defence that could not be disproved. She survived her imprisonment by about six months, after which she suddenly dropped dead, perhaps one of the unattributed casualties of the night of 31st January-1st February 1953.

Of the various public utilities, electricity supplies had been among the worst hit. The gale which blew before the surge had already blown down overhead low voltage lines before the sea struck, but the flooding attacked more severely the underground cables in urban areas. When flood water entered houses where the mains had not been turned off—and few householders had the presence of mind to take this precaution at times like those—the service cables simply burned out. In other cases, water penetrated the paper insulation of the cables and made them useless. Meters immersed in salt water for only a brief period were rendered beyond repair. And there was a good deal of damage too, of course, to the supply network itself. Electricity men at Harwich, for example, were faced with the failure of five of the town's major sub-stations, one of which was completely submerged by flood water. Some 1,150 premises had had their supplies cut off. At the same time, there were urgent requests for extra installations to floodlight sea defence repair work and priority calls to restore supplies to water and sewage pumping

*In this one instance only, I have used a fictitious name.

stations. It was important, too, to visit flooded householders and warn them not to use appliances that had been submerged until they had been checked.

The first priority in the towns was to restore supplies to sewage and water stations, gasworks and street lighting. Some 600 volunteers came in from unaffected parts of the Eastern Electricity Board's area, and from the London Board, to help in the work, which was organised for some time on a three-shift basis. Within three weeks of the disaster, supplies had been restored to all but a tiny proportion of the cut-off premises, and work on those remaining had been withheld, as at Jack Loveday's house in Great Yarmouth and Mrs Vincent's in Harwich, at the request of the health authorities. In all, in the Eastern Electricity Board's area, forty-one sub-stations, eighteen transformers, 6,000 yards of service cable, over 6,500 meters and hundreds of pieces of subsidiary equipment had to be replaced or substantially repaired.

The process of clearing up the mess after the flood was particularly delicate for the workers at the Bramble Island explosives factory, where Leonard Gostling and Donald Harris carried out the vain rescue attempt described in Chapter Three. Over a thousand men were employed to rebuild the sea wall round the factory, but this was only the beginning: there then remained the tricky problem of disposing of hundreds of tons of explosives rendered useless—and, even worse, unstable—by their immersion. Eventually, it was decided to sink them at sea. The explosives were manhandled from the magazines for over half a mile to a concrete barge, and in June this was towed out to sea by two fishing boats with two employees, Donald Rumble and Ronald Ranson, on board. The two men (who were later awarded the B.E.M. for their part in this tricky operation) then scuttled the barge by opening the sea-cocks, and joined the fishing boats.

"We moved away to what we thought was a safe distance," Mr Rumble remembers, "and watched with binoculars. The barge took about an hour to go down. The spot was marked with a Trinity House buoy and none of the explosives has ever floated back to the surface."

But all this was in the future. As things stood in that first week in February, the coastal population of eastern England was in a state of severe shock. Even those who had not been physically affected had seen the unimaginable happen before their very eyes. Families had been broken up and billetted wherever room could be found: children from Kings Lynn fifty miles away at Rushden, 3,000 people from Mablethorpe twenty miles away at Louth, another 1,500 from Sutton-on-Sea at Alford. And for many—from the American servicemen who, so far from the usual pattern of things, had lost their wives or children in a strange land, to the Ridleys, with only a wrecked home to go back to—it was a matter of picking up the pieces, glad to be alive, and hoping for the best.

KJJ 960

CHAPTER FIVE

AFTER the storm, the reckoning; and it was not long before the people of eastern England began to wonder why there was no official warning of the impending disaster and whether the aftermath was handled as well as it might have been.

At first, there were cheering signs of the sort of national togetherness that was familiar in wartime. Florence Ridley's experience, quoted in Chapter Four, of the wealth of succour extended to the Sea Palling refugees was typical. And as news of the disaster began to appear in the papers there was an overwhelming response to the plight of the east coast. The British public, long accustomed to responding to appeals for help for victims of natural disasters in countries it has hardly heard of, is rarely called upon to succour victims of similar circumstances nearer home. On this occasion, the flood of gifts became a positive embarrassment to the local helpers who had to cope with it. Edward Sillett, in charge of the Cavendish Hotel reception centre in Felixstowe, remembers that "the W.V.S. collected so much clothing that we had to store the surplus in another hall . . . We had more offers to accommodate the flooded than we could use . . . People came from all over East Anglia to help . . . A young woman set up a free laundry service in the amusement park and an elderly woman brought down her week's ration of food to be distributed . . . The baker sent pastries, bread and cooked meat . . . " Within a few days, warehouses all over eastern England were stocked with countless items of clothing which could not yet be handed out because there was nowhere for the recipients to keep it. Shortly afterwards, lorry-loads of furniture started to arrive, with the result that on 9th February Sir David Maxwell-Fyfe, Home Secretary, was forced to make a statement in the House of Commons encouraging donors of furniture to channel it through their local W.V.S. Additionally, local flood relief funds soon began to swell with contributions from inland Rotary Clubs, Womens' Institutes, Townswomens' Guilds, pub collections and the like. And there were countless individual, often very moving gestures: food parcels and packets of sweets from well-wishers all over the country and abroad, gifts whose storage and distribution in fact added to the headaches of the voluntary organisations. The Scripture Gift Mission, perhaps recalling the parable of the widow's mite, offered copies of the tract *Words of Comfort* for distribution to the parishioners of St John's, Lowestoft, the church where Detective-Constable Sparkes carried out the rescue described in Chapter Two.

⇦ The Police throughout the flood area coped with a great variety of tasks quietly and efficiently. Here another Canvey Island survivor is carried to safety. *Press Association*

There was also a good deal of local self-help from such organisations as the Scouts, Junior St John Ambulance Brigades, and church youth clubs. Margaret Wright, then fifteen, remembers how as a member of a youth group "I helped every weekend to clear the mud from homes" at Harwich: "It was a heart-breaking job. I particularly remember an old man's beloved piano, standing in his front room, completely ruined." Like many others who remember the flood and its aftermath, Margaret Wright recalls the succour afforded by the Salvation Army, who, it is perhaps worth noting, did not need to go into committee before they found what needed to be done and setting about doing it. The Army was providing hot drinks and soup to the emergency sea defence repair gangs within a few hours of the disaster; within a few days, it was so well organised as to be able to offer a mobile hot coffee service to volunteer groups such as that to which Margaret Wright belonged: a case of deeds which contrasts sharply with the words that, about the same time, were being mouthed in the House of Commons.

A less pleasing aspect of human nature was illustrated by sporadic outbreaks of looting in areas from which shopkeepers and residents had been evacuated, despite police reinforcements sent to these areas not only to deter looters but also to keep residents away until it was safe for them to return. There was also a certain amount of trouble with parties of sightseers, though

The supply of clothing for flood victims was so generous that it became an embarrassment. Here, relief workers sort through contributions at a rest centre at South Benfleet.

Press Association

The bitter weather, the mud, and the heavy work made mobile canteens a godsend to repair gangs working against time to mend the breaches in the sea defences before the next high tide. The Red Cross were among the voluntary bodies to organise refreshments, among many other duties. *Walmsley and Webb*

not as much, no doubt, as there would be in the car-owning society of today, or if disaster had struck at any other time but midwinter.

But as is the way of things, the public who responded so generously at first to the plight of eastern England fairly soon lost interest and returned to its own affairs, especially as 1953 was, among other things, Coronation year, and much local endeavour was mortgaged to preparations for suitable celebrations. Pictures of churches and farms apparently floating in the sea made for dramatic front page newspaper pictures; but once the water receded the Press, quite understandably, turned its attention to other matters. In fact, the agony of the east coast went on—well into the spring and summer, and in some areas even longer. The plight of the evacuated families from Hunstanton, Snettisham, Sea Palling, Great Yarmouth, Felixstowe, Harwich, Clacton, Canvey and Foulness was in many cases more shattering than that of wartime evacuees. The latter had at least some warning and were able to take a suitcase with them. When the sea bursts into your home in the middle of the night, however, you do not wait to assemble a change of underwear, your toothbrush and flannel, your insurance policies and bank book, or even your spectacles and dentures. In any case, the sheer pressure of time and space forced rescuers in some places to put an embargo on anything but human cargo. The result was that many of the evacuees were virtually destitute, torn ruthlessly from their homes with no knowledge of when they would be able to go back. As Hilda Grieve commented in her exhaustive study of the disaster as it affected Essex: "The sea's achievement in one night challenges comparison with that of the Luftwaffe in six years," so far as the accommodation of evacuees at short notice was concerned; the responsibility fell on a Civil Defence service which existed, after eight years of peace, only in rudimentary and stood-down form.

Probably no one imagined—least of all the evacuees—that the people who took flight on the night of 31st January might not see their homes again for months. But within a couple of days it became clear that the occupants of the overnight rest centres would have to be rehoused temporarily elsewhere.

Many went to stay with friends or relations, but those who remained became the responsibility of the local authorities, whose staff had to engage in a thankless task which many of them remembered only too well from the outbreak of the Second World War—the weary trek in search of billets. Edward Sillett's experience in Felixstowe of having more offers than evacuees was not echoed generally; and for the first few days after the flood, the work of billeting officers was hampered by the refusal of the government to reintroduce any kind of official billeting subsidy such as had been in operation during the war. Even when the government gave way as a result of pressure from M.P.s for the affected areas, the concession was so hedged about with conditions that it did nothing to relieve the distress of families which, one might have thought, had suffered enough. The establishment might make its public gestures, such as heart-warming speeches in the Commons and the frequent visits of members of the royal family to affected areas, but it could not bring itself to see the plight of the thousands of homeless in any other terms than those of bureaucracy. A Ministry of Housing and Local Government circular sent out a week after the disaster authorised the payment of a billeting allowance, but added that this was to cover the cost of lodging only; as for food, the evacuees must make their own arrangements and apply to the National Assistance Board if in need. It may well be wondered what effect this news had on the self-sufficient people of East Anglia. It is perhaps significant that although most of the people I have spoken to or corresponded with in the writing of this book pay fulsome tributes to local individuals, officials and voluntary organisations, none (with the notable exception of farmers, of whom more later) had a good word for the government of the day. In so far as the government and its ministries appear in the story (which is in truth, with the honourable exception of the Ministry of Agriculture and Fisheries, not very much) they are remembered as obstructions, failing to comprehend the scale of the disaster or to appreciate the depth of human suffering involved.

It was not surprising that, in the circumstances, rumours, true and false, about the ways of bureaucracy flourished during the first days after the flood—and in some cases for a good deal longer. One story that swept Harwich, for example, was that anyone whose electricity meter had been damaged would have to pay for a new one—false. But it was true enough that one Harwich pensioner who had lost his cheap tobacco tokens in the turmoil received a reply from officials sharply drawing his attention to the rules governing the loss of these tokens and the fact that he would have to do without until the next series started in September. And there were problems, too, for those who had lost National Health spectacles or false teeth. One of these was Mrs Vincent of Harwich, who remembers that in the days after the flood she and her neighbours, "who were all getting a bit long in the tooth, used to meet up at a snack bar—no teeth and no specs—what a sight!"

Caravans and huts were home for six months for many Harwich flood victims. Mrs A. M. Vincent, whose story is told in this book, was one of the residents on this site while her house was being repaired. She, her husband, her daughter and her son occupied one caravan, with a shed beside it so that her husband and son, both engine-drivers on shift work, could sleep when they were off shift. *Mrs A. M. Vincent*

Thus it was that large numbers of people who on Saturday 31st January 1953 had been looking forward to the turn of the year in their own homes, planning their new season's plantings and perhaps putting up some new wallpaper in the living-room, were two weeks later in the unwelcome position of having to negotiate their own terms with their temporary landladies or, even worse, contemplating spending several weeks—perhaps months—in such premises as "an old prisoner-of-war camp some ten miles away from Canvey at Langdon Hills, owned by the Shell Petroleum Company, with room for about 450 people", which came up for discussion at one local emergency committee meeting. One of the revelations of the disaster for the people of the east coast was that, in areas of life where governments are expected to govern, people are on their own.

Difficulties over the immediate subsistence of evacuated families were quickly followed by questions of compensation. East Anglia was—and in some parts still is—an area where people live pretty well from hand to mouth, with little left over for such luxuries as insurance, and many of those whose homes were wrecked or damaged were, in fact, uninsured. Bearing in mind that 24,000 homes were damaged, the total of £1½ millions claimed on insurance—an average of about £60 per home—is indicative. Many people had suffered damage which was incapable of being assessed: the possible loss of summer holiday lettings, losses from hens that went off lay or cows whose milk yield had been disturbed, and so on. Even those who were insured soon became familiar with the sound well-known to anyone who has ever had to make an insurance claim, the sound of insurance men rustling through the small print, taking in premiums being an activity that insurance companies like more than paying out claims. And then, of course, many householders, especially the older ones, had not altered the values insured since before the war. "New-for-old" policies did not then exist, and many people were shocked at the assessments placed upon their treasured furniture—assessments which were, of course, quite inadequate for replacements of the same quality. Nor did the insurance companies display great finesse in arriving at their settlements.

"Those assessing the damage caused by the waters to household property," said an insurance journal afterwards, "found that a rough yardstick was to assume that one-third of a person's property was in his upstairs rooms and two-thirds downstairs. From all reports this basis proved to be most accurate in the majority of cases. A typical householder's comprehensive claim settlement went something like this: sum assured under the policy, £600. In the upstairs rooms, untouched, was, say, £200 worth of furniture and fittings. Using the one third-two thirds basis, that left £400 worth of property downstairs. In such circumstances the claim was settled for a figure of the order of £420." Despite the self-congratulatory tone of all this, insurance problems were significant enough to cause a question to be asked in the House of Commons, to which the Home Secretary replied that "the government have no reason to doubt that in this situation the insurance interests have acted, and will act, in accordance with the high tradition and reputation which they have in these matters". One of the preoccupations of the industrial (which means, in insurance jargon, door-to-door) section of the business during the weeks following the floods was nevertheless to trace evacuated policyholders so that weekly payments could be kept up. Against what eventuality these payments were solicited must be a matter of conjecture. Christopher Manser of Canvey Island recalls that the family's insurance company refused to pay out on the deaths of his three brothers on the grounds that they were caused by an Act of God, "and we had to borrow money to bury them". And some possessions, of course, were not insurable. There was, for instance, the £900 worth of used one pound bank notes, kept safe from the taxman, that floated out into the North Sea down the back of an armchair, never to be seen again unless, perhaps, by a lucky beachcomber.

The Lord Mayor of London's Relief Fund, opened on the Monday following the disaster, was aimed primarily at the relief of personal distress and at the compensation of those who had suffered personal loss or damage not recoverable from insurance. It had the advantage over a government

Exactly one month after the disaster work proceeds on clearing the marshes and repairing the banks at Burnham Overy Staithe. But it was to be years before the farmland was back to normal.
Gilbert White

scheme, as the Lord Mayor pointed out more than once, that it was more flexible; changes in the situation, needing fresh action, could be responded to at once instead of having to go through the tortuous channels of bureaucracy, of which the people of eastern England were already having their fill. The division of responsibility worked out was that the payment of compensation would be handled by the Fund, while the government agreed to meet the cost of emergency repairs, the restoration of the sea-defences and the restoration of agricultural land.

"It is clear," Churchill told the House of Commons on Monday, 2nd February, "that the catastrophe is one which will require to be treated upon a national basis and, broadly, as a national responsibility." It was later announced that the government would match the Lord Mayor's Fund pound for pound—a promise that led many organisers of local funds to submit their collections to London in the belief that the victims would thereby obtain greater benefits; but a promise that was not in the event kept, only just over £2 millions being given by the government as against the public's £7¼ millions—another blot on the government's handling of the whole disaster. When the Fund was wound up in 1956, the then Chancellor of the Exchequer gave a sort of qualified half-promise—one can put it no higher than that—that the extra money would be kept in reserve against some future disaster; this was, naturally, the last that was ever heard of it. It was not, for example, produced with suitable interest at the time of Aberfan.

It was inevitable—it is endemic to public relief funds of this kind—that there should have been some disputes over the handling of the fund at local level. When flood victims read in the papers of the ready public response to the Lord Mayor's appeal they became impatient to see the colour of the money—not unnaturally since many were living from day to day on doles from the National Assistance Board. When it was announced that local flood relief committees could make emergency grants of up to £25 from the fund, this discretionary power was widely interpreted as a right. Unruly queues formed at council offices, to become even more unruly when it was discovered that entitlement to the grant was subject to something suspiciously like a means test. It seems likely that officials were over-zealous in their desire for proof of need, especially bearing in mind that many of the recipients were still in a state of shock, to which their privations in temporary quarters after the flood and worries over money had added extra strain. But there was also a completely understandable official sense of responsibility towards publicly-subscribed money which would probably still be evident today regardless of the comparative profligacy, especially in the social services, of contemporary local government. Whatever the rights and wrongs of the matter, there were arguments, there was some resentment, there were even fights between claimants and officials; and they could have been avoided if the prevailing mood of those responsible for grants had been to find reasons for handing them out rather than reasons for holding them back.

Later, when settlements for compensation began to be made, there were more misgivings. Neighbours compared their cheques and some felt cheated. Some people were thought to have made out of the disaster; as one Norfolk housewife (not herself involved in a claim) told me, "There were some that got this carpeted and that carpeted — they'd never had carpets before". Other people were held to have jumped the queue, and in some areas net curtains were a-twitch all day if the compensation official made an appearance in the street in case he should be seen not to be calling in strict order.

One of those who had a brush with this official was Anne Smith of Shottisham, Suffolk. The ground floor of their home had been flooded and they had eventually escaped from a bedroom window. Downstairs, their linoleum, a settee, two armchairs, a radio and a nearly new pram were ruined. While Mrs Smith was staying with her mother to let the house dry out, the compensation official called, totted up his figures, and made an offer of £17. "I'll never forget what my mother did," Mrs Smith said afterwards. "She had the most furious row. She called him just about everything. We got £17 out of them. I'll bet he'll never forget her."

Particular hardship was felt by owners of seaside bungalows and boarding-house landladies who wanted to get their rooms ready for re-letting in the summer. The special problem here was that buildings which have been immersed in salt water have to be dried out thoroughly before redecoration can be started; otherwise, stains keep on coming through. The decision on this is not one that can be made by eye alone; and indeed residues of the salt immersion of 1953 can still be seen on my own bedroom wall in north Norfolk after twenty-three years, two redecorations, and the most earnest advice of local builders. But eventually, it was agreed that people who wanted to redecorate could take their cash on the nail on the understanding that if the new paints and papers deteriorated they would have to stand this further loss themselves. Many householders chose to take the money, not only so that they could get their summer lettings but also for the sake of the morale-boosting effect of fresh decorations. Some later regretted their decision.

One continuing result of the 1953 floods is that many houses along the eastern coastal strip remain difficult to keep in good decorative order since the effect of a soaking in salt is almost permanent. This also explains why many houses in the area have been given an inner skin of plasterboard battened to the true inner wall, a fact which may or may not be revealed by vendors, and may or may not be detected by surveyors. Other houses where this precaution has not been taken continue to show a tell-tale brown stain within days of redecoration.

Wednesday, 4th February, and in Korndyke Road, Canvey, the flood waters have receded. But there is still urgent work to be done, and for Kenneth Dawson, local R.S.P.C.A. representative, this means a terrified pig to be rescued. It was found floating on a bed in a flooded bungalow, one of many animals that the surge lifted into pig legend. *Press Association*

It is only fair to say, however, that many people were well satisfied with the compensation they received. Among these was Jack Loveday of Great Yarmouth, who remembers: "Such damage as had been done to our furniture was repairable and paid by the Norfolk Flood Relief Fund, and there was also a voucher system by means of which one could acquire various items of furniture, bedding and so on." The Lovedays were also given a hundredweight of coal to help with drying out the house. Madeleine Swinn of Wells, who was able to return home after three months, "when workmen began making the place safe and our furniture and goods were returned bit by bit as they were repaired", adds: "One didn't count the loss — at least we were alive."

But not everyone on the east coast was as well-satisfied as Mr Loveday and Mrs Swinn. At Harwich, residents in the Bathside area, which had been worst hit in January, were still waiting in September for essential repairs to their houses. At 3 Albert Street, Mrs A. M. Vincent and her family had been given a certificate in July permitting them to return to their home. But as September opened, and another winter loomed, many Bathside houses remained virtually as they had been in the days after the flood. Mrs Vincent was one of the organisers of a petition to the local council which complained of ceilings left unplastered, cracks and holes in walls not filled, and rotting mounds of bedding and other rubbish left festering for over six months. Some families were still living in their upstairs rooms. Local builders' claims that the delays were due partly to the shortage of plasterers lost some of their credibility when it was noted that men had been taken off the work of repairing houses to restore the Masonic Hall. As she collected names for her petition — eventually over 300 — Mrs Vincent went round the area with a reporter from the local paper, the *Harwich and Dovercourt Standard.* She pointed out to him "a heap of straw in the backyard of an unoccupied house. 'The dead bodies of chickens and rabbits are still under that straw', she said, while one of the housewives from a neighbouring house said that until recently a dead dog had been lying in the yard, which had no gate and was entirely open to children playing in the area". Mrs Vincent told the Press that already she and her family were having to spend the evenings in their overcoats, or go to bed at eight o'clock. There were spaces of three and four inches between inside doors and the walls. Rats infested the bedding and other rubbish still lying about. It was no joke that the film currently showing at the Regent, Dovercourt was called "Remains to be Seen".

The petition worked wonders, Mrs Vincent, now in her seventies, remembers. News of it appeared in the local papers on Friday, 4th September. On Monday morning, a firm brought in from Ipswich started work in Bathside. But it was never satisfactorily explained why repairs at Bathside had taken so long; why the Harwich sanitary authorities had cleared for rehabilitation houses where there was, a few weeks later, to be an outbreak of typhoid; why the attempts of landlords to put their property to rights were held back by what one of them, Leonard Rose, described in a letter to the *Harwich and Dovercourt Standard* (4th September 1953), as "hindrances and delays from government departments"; or why, whatever the shortage of skilled tradesmen, basic clearing-up work to remove visible health hazards had been left undone over seven months after the flood.

In contrast to the problems of the residents of Bathside, Harwich, however, the farmers I have spoken to have no complaints about the way they were treated by the Ministry of Agriculture.

Charles Ramm of Wells considers that the Ministry's attitude was "very fair", not only as regards compensation for the loss of stock but also in terms of help towards restoring the pastures. Although the marshes near Wells that Mr Ramm used were left idle in 1953 and could be used only to a limited extent during the following year, there were ample supplies of gypsum available, he remembers, to be ploughed in to offset the effects of the salt. Nevertheless, Mr Ramm reckons that it was ten years before the farming side of his business recovered from the blow of 1953. Fortunately for him, he had his retail butchery business to sustain him and his family.

Harris Wroth, farming 600 acres in partnership with two brothers at Holkham, goes even further in his praise of government support. "We thought it was hard at the time," he told me, "but in a sense it was one of the best things that ever happened to the marshes. We had so much help from the advisory people. About eighteen months after the floods the marshes recovered, but we decided to plough and re-seed. Now we're getting far better grasses than ever before." Mr Wroth's neighbour, Peter Hancock, was equally happy with the compensation for the loss of use of the marsh, which in his case lasted for four years. The most enduring effect of the floods that he noticed was that until recently the shrubbery in front of his farmhouse was difficult to maintain. It seemed that deep-rooting shrubs suffered a setback once their roots reached down to the salt; but now, he told me, even the shrubs seem to have re-established themselves.

On one issue, however, most people along the east coast seem to be agreed: "We should have been warned." On the face of it, they have a good case. It was 5.30 p.m. on Saturday when the sea broke through at Sutton-on-Sea in Lincolnshire. The flooding at Kings Lynn and the breaches at Snettisham, Heacham, Hunstanton and Holme came about an hour later. Wells, Cley and Salthouse succumbed at about eight according to official accounts, though Madeleine Swinn puts it three hours earlier at Wells. And so on round the coast, until it was after midnight when the surge reached Harwich, Clacton, Jaywick, Foulness and Canvey Island.

Ironically, it was those places where the loss of life was greatest, and which were most vulnerable since the surge was not due to reach them until their inhabitants were in bed, that had most chance of warning if there had been any mechanism for giving one.

However, it would be unfair to let hindsight lead one into too critical a view of the authorities, whatever might have been the popular sentiment of the time. Charles Goodey, former Lowestoft reporter for the *East Anglian Daily Times*, expressed the popular view when he commented in 1973 that: "There was ample warning as the flood level hit various spots further north that it was moving south, and ample time for precautions to have been taken to minimise the damage. It was a disaster that should never have happened. No one apparently had the commonsense to pass flood warnings down the coast, so each place hit by the flood was taken by surprise." The jury at the inquest on the Canvey Island victims actually added a rider to similar effect. But the fact was that in 1953 there was no mechanism by which warnings could have been issued. No doubt the critics had in mind a warning system on the lines of wartime Civil Defence, in 1953 still a vivid memory. But even if the wartime system had not by 1953 been dismantled, it is doubtful whether it could have been effective in an entirely different set of circumstances. Even on a simpler level, "passing warnings down the coast" would have been impossible in practical terms since telephone lines were among the first casualties of the flood—indeed, Mablethorpe police knew nothing of the flood at the adjacent village of Sutton-on-Sea until the sea-wall burst open in front of their own station—and in any case anyone in a position to pass a warning message was otherwise engaged in rescue work. Given that it was the first time such an emergency had arisen in peacetime since the apparatus of modern com-

Grim evidence of the havoc wrought by the flood, revealed by the R.A.F.'s aerial survey. This was the scene at Mablethorpe, Lincolnshire, where the night's largest single breach of the sea-defences was made. *Crown Copyright*

munications became available, it seems difficult to sustain the criticism, however much one understands the shock and distress that prompted it. As will be seen in the next chapter, the warning system devised in 1953 in the light of the disaster, and subsequently brought up to date, has in fact passed one test "for real" with some success.

Turning now to the official response to the disaster, it seems that, given the lack of warning, this was as swift and effective as could have been expected, except at government level. The picture changes, of course, according to the area involved. Urban districts were best off. According to Bertie Hart's account, the Borough Engineer at Kings Lynn arrived at the police station, having rounded up his foremen, almost as soon as any danger was evident. Clacton, Lowestoft, Felixstowe, Harwich and other towns, too, were able to muster their resources quickly, mainly because their well-staffed police stations provided a focal point. It is striking, though, that the smaller communities, for example the stricken stretch of coast between Kings Lynn and Hunstanton, were dependent upon their own resources of voluntary help, together with the local constables, for many hours; and at Sea Palling local people deserved most of the credit for the night's rescues. The story was much the same on the more isolated parts of the Suffolk and Essex coasts. In these areas, emergency services are thin on the ground, the police more noticeably so now even than in 1953, and it is significant that these were the places where such voluntary organisations as the Red Cross, the St John Ambulance and the W.V.S. tend to come into the story much earlier than in the better-endowed urban districts, where their role was supportive rather than primary.

But much has changed since 1953. Then, the physical pattern of Civil Defence still existed in rudimentary form, and, more important perhaps, the wartime spirit of community consciousness was still lingering on. The sense of public duty, amounting almost to an instinct, which led Bertie Hart to go to the police station as soon as he heard of trouble, and H. W. Temple Cole of Snettisham to swing into the organisation of a rescue team on the spot, may not be so deeply implanted today; yet, on the other hand, there now exists in all the vulnerable areas a master plan under a co-ordinated control which takes into account such sources of voluntary help as might be available. The other marked difference is that in 1953 there were huge numbers of National Servicemen in East Anglia and the East Midlands who could be called in at short notice for rescue and repair operations, together with a large number of service camps, still partially occupied or kept on a "care and maintenance" basis which could be pressed into duty as emergency rest centres or at least as a source of emergency feeding. These reserves of manpower and accommodation no longer exist. Within days of the 1953 disaster, there were thousands of men at work on the Suffolk sea-defences; today, Suffolk can muster about 400 men from its own resources—but then where would it turn? In 1953, Suffolk was chequered with service stations in a reasonable state of repair and many of them active; now, there are seven active units. But on the plus side, changes, discussed in the next chapter, have also come over the national organisation of emergency services.

The timing of the 1953 flood was critical. The surge reached the most vulnerable stretch of coastline — the Essex coast — at a time which might have been calculated to cause the greatest loss of life. As was noted in Chapter One, the flood of 1897, though it caused considerable damage, occurred in the daytime and no lives were lost. That it was a *Saturday* night, and a Saturday night at one of the quietest times of the year, is also important; on a Saturday night in midwinter, it's still possible to drive for miles outside East Anglia's towns without meeting another car. The scope for natural communication by word of mouth is limited. But it is only right to mention the dissentient voice of farmer Harris Wroth of Holkham, who told me: "Thank God it didn't happen in daylight." The loss of life, he believes, would have been enormous in the Wells area earlier in the day, since so many more people would have been about to be overwhelmed like the sheep, the geese and the pheasants which eventually finished up in the trees.

What of the long-term implications of the government's reaction to 1953? It is clear that in the matter of compensation and rehabilitation the government's record runs some way behind that of the general public and of the voluntary organisations. Only the farmers seem to have been satisfied. The most notable failure of the government was its reneging on its "pound for pound" promise, as a result of which many local relief funds were made over to the Lord Mayor's appeal in the belief that the net result to their communities would thereby be enhanced. They were trapped by Churchill's resounding, but empty, words about "national responsibility" which they believed to be an acceptance of government liability instead of, as it turned out, merely a slogan to stimulate national sacrifice. This is a blot, albeit a small one, on Churchill's record as a peacetime minister; but it calls into question a much larger issue, which is this: to what extent we are, in times of crisis, members one of another? There should surely have been no need for pensioners to send off their five-shilling postal orders, infant school children to make collections, or old ladies to go through their chests of drawers to see what might be spared for the flood victims. We were in 1953, and still are despite current economic troubles, one of the world's more affluent nations. Governments then, as now, had no compunction in allocating funds to causes rather less worthy than relief of the suffering of a sizeable proportion of their own people. We were, and are, as well able to finance the cost of natural disasters completely, without recourse to public charity, as to finance, for example, a war — and to do so without unnecessary conditions or delays. There is no doubt, however, that if a comparable disaster were to occur tomorrow, the victims would again be dependent for succour upon public charity, administered by grey-suited men with bureaucratic minds, who would later queue up for their honours. It is scarcely worth pointing out that the five million pounds withheld by the government in 1953 when it broke its "pound for pound" pledge would by now, allowing for even the most modest rate of interest, have provided a useful emergency fund for the next Lynmouth, or Aberfan, or East Coast flood. The pledge, if such it was, was merely words across the floor of the Commons. It is when government is most needed that you can test its worth.

The crossroads at Burnham Overy Town, over two miles from the sea — but only a few yards from the River Burn. Flood water funnelled up the river, bursting the banks and leaving driftwood and animal carcases high in the trees. *Gilbert White*

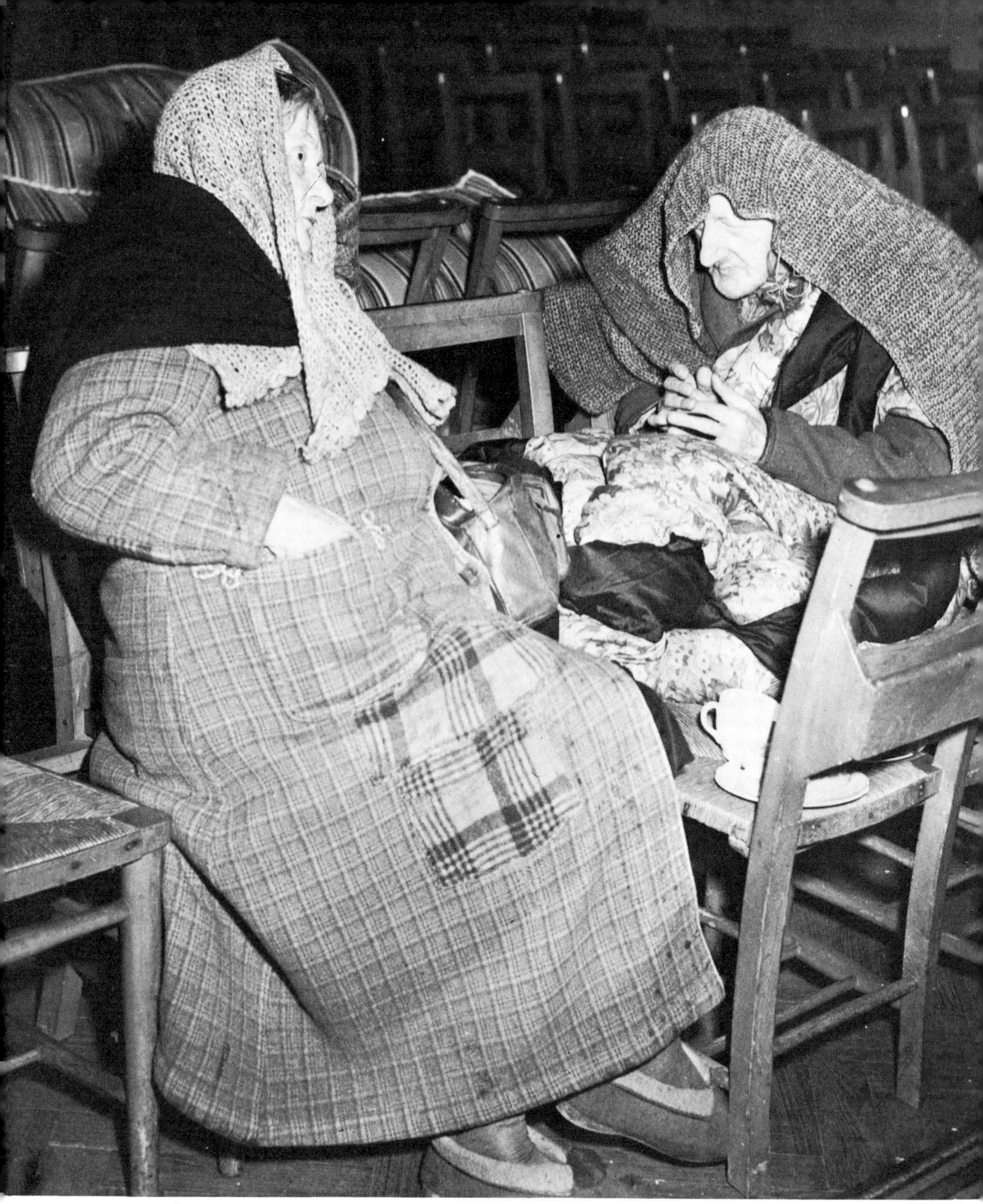

Refugees from Canvey Island sheltering at a hastily-organised rest centre at Benfleet Methodist Church on Sunday morning. The blind and crippled old man on the right was to discover later that his home had been completely destroyed. *Press Association*

CHAPTER SIX

COULD it happen again?

This is a question never far from the minds of the people of the east coast who remember the devastation and loss of life in 1953. In the wild, dark nights of midwinter, especially along the less well-protected shores, it's a question that can assume urgency amounting almost to panic. But this is, in a way, a good thing: the lesson of 1953 was a cruel one, but one hard to forget. Nowadays, in eastern England, a gale isn't just a gale; it's a potential threat to be watched carefully.

The simple answer to the question, however, is that the physical conditions that produced the 1953 disaster could happen again and almost certainly will, at least once more before the end of this century. Some danger exists throughout autumn and winter—the national storm warning service introduced after 1953 operates from mid-September to the end of April—but December and January are the most critical months. It is then that the wind is most likely to come from the north or north-west, and given the volatile atmospheric conditions that led to the formation of 1953's depression Low Z there are some five or six periods of spring tides when the coast is especially vulnerable.

Of course, much has changed since 1953, and the most significant change has been in official recognition of the hazard, of which the national warning service is the symbol. It will be remembered that in 1953 there was no mechanism by which meteorological forecasts could be linked with hydrographic information to produce a warning of impending floods. The official report into the 1953 disaster recommended that a warning system should be set up, combining both meteorological and hydrographic information, and this now operates as an independent unit, run by naval hydrographers, at the Meteorological Office headquarters at Bracknell throughout the autumn and winter. Its warnings are based on tidal readings at key points from Scotland to the Thames Estuary, combined with Meteorological Office weather forecasts and the records of previous surges. From Bracknell, warnings go out to county police headquarters and the river divisions of water authorities. The east coast is divided into five sections, and the aim is to give any of the sections at least a twelve-hour warning, ranging in severity from "provisional" to "danger". Both the police forces and the river divisions strengthen the system locally, as will be seen later in this chapter, on the basis of their own tidal readings and local wisdom.

One of the results of the fresh assessment of the danger following 1953 was the discovery that about a million Londoners living in riverside areas from Barking to Twickenham would be at risk if the full force of a North Sea surge were to drive up the Thames. The flood of January 1928, which drowned fourteen people in central London, was merely a hint of the potential for disaster. In 1953, the wind driving the surge swung away over western Europe early enough to avoid grievous damage along the Thames, though there was some flooding along the outer reaches of the estuary. But the direct result of 1953 was to put some muscle into the long-mooted scheme for a Thames flood prevention barrier. At the time of writing, this is due to be completed in 1980, at a cost which has already topped £400 millions and will no doubt go higher. Meanwhile, the chances of a flood in central London are officially estimated at about fifty to one, while low-lying areas upstream, such as Twickenham, Richmond and Chiswick, are considerably more vulnerable. The Greater London Council, like all other local authorities in vulnerable areas, has its own flood warning system, with contingency plans for the evacuation of areas at risk. The warning system involves the use of air-raid sirens, announcements over London's three local radio stations and the use of police loudspeaker vans.

Residents in coastal areas of Lincolnshire, Norfolk, Suffolk and Essex might well note with some cynicism the detail and money invested in flood prevention in London. For the east coast counties, the problem will remain a permanent one. There can be no hope of flood *prevention*; people must learn to live with the threat.

Planning for another 1953-type surge is in the hands of the county councils, whose emergency planning teams are responsible not only for potential floods but also for such other major incidents as pollution from traffic or factory accidents involving dangerous chemicals or oil, oil leakages from shipwrecked tankers, major aircraft or rail crashes, and so on up the scale of disaster as far as (and including) nuclear war.

The emergency planning officers and their teams are the legatees of the old Civil Defence system, which was bedevilled from its inception in the 1930s by political scrimshanking. Even today, there are Labour councillors in the East End of London—a traditionally anti-Civil Defence area, despite the lessons of the Blitz and the fact that the area's wartime sufferings were, in some boroughs, considerably worsened by lack of local government co-operation in pre-war plans—who refuse to participate in flood prevention exercises, presumably on the grounds that they are a cover for something more sinister. But I am told that such attitudes are unknown elsewhere in the flood-prone area, and that in any case elected members have a merely supportive and relatively minor role in local authorities' emergency plans, which respond to (and are partly paid for by) the Home Office and are designed to be operated by the paid officials and the emergency services.

Many of the operations rooms maintained by the emergency planners are indeed the bombproof centres set up for Civil Defence in the 1950s and subsequently much hounded and picketed by the nuclear disarmament movement. And it must be said that the planners themselves, many of them retired service officers, are slightly worrying people to talk to. It is always unnerving to sit drinking coffee discussing unthinkables with men professionally trained to cultivate a relaxed manner at all times, especially when their bookshelves are full of manuals on the effects of nuclear warfare and file copies of a periodical forbiddingly called *Survival.* There are, too, points in the conversation where the eyes tend to glaze over and pregnant silences fall. It is not unimaginable, for example, that eastern England could be affected by a flood so severe that the normal processes of government and law and order might break down. Such possibilities are perhaps nearer the surface than most of us realise. But I was unable to find out from any source what plans there might be for such a contingency, beyond the fact that a battle order exists for the movement of limited numbers of troops to affected areas. (The scope for such military intervention is, of course, strictly limited in view of the run-down

Sunday morning in Kings Lynn, and an R.A.F. team rescues householders who were marooned in their upstairs rooms for fifteen hours. The level reached by the flood water can be seen on the wall beside the door on the extreme right of the picture.

state of the armed forces, and much smaller than in 1953 when there was a huge reserve of manpower among national servicemen.) And some local authorities were clearly not anxious to reveal or discuss their plans for the routine warning or evacuation of flooded areas, much less for preventing the breakdown of normal life.

Other authorities take the sensible view that the more preparation people have, the less will be the pressure on the emergency services if their plans have to be put into operation. In Essex, the responsibility for emergency planning rests with Group Captain Richard Bowen, who in 1976 was masterminding his plans in a converted shop in the shadow of the County Hall at Chelmsford. Group Captain Bowen's area includes Canvey Island, where there were fifty-eight deaths in 1953, and the industrial belt stretching along the north bank of the Thames Estuary as far as the Greater London border, a strip of development rich in oil and chemical installations. His file contains contingency plans for anything, as he says, "from a leaking oil tanker up to a full tank war", taking in a repetition of 1953 on the way.

Not unnaturally, the focus of his attention as far as floods are concerned is Canvey Island, scene of the historic evacuation of some 11,000 people in 1953 but now with a permanent population three times as large. Now, as then, there is in addition a proportion of chalets and holiday homes occupied only in the summer.

One of the problems in 1953, when police and local volunteers were racing against time in conditions whose outcome they dared not imagine, was that there was no accurate picture of the possible numbers to be rescued. A good deal of the rescuers' time was spent in trying to arouse people who were, in fact, safe at home elsewhere. Today, the local council maintains an annual register of the population, with a separate list of the housebound or infirm, and each home is circulated at the start of the danger season with instructions on emergency procedure. Given the existence of the warning system—Canvey could expect a minimum of two hours' warning—the possibilities for self-help are greater than in 1953, says Group Captain Bowen, not only because of the wider availability of private cars but also because a larger proportion of the homes on the island are two-storey houses rather than bungalows.

There are only two exits from Canvey. In the event of a flood threat, these could become choked, preventing the arrival of emergency services and repair crews. So there is a permanently signposted route to separate evacuees from incoming relief traffic, so devised that it can be operated with a minimum of police supervision.

What would happen in the event of a flood threat to Canvey is this. The warning from Bracknell would go direct to the police and then to the emergency plans team at Chelmsford, one member of which is on standby throughout the year. The Essex River Division of the Anglian Water Authority, which is responsible for sea-defences, and the emergency officers of the fourteen local districts involved would also be alerted. At each stage of alert, a widening number of people and organisations would be brought into the emergency circle, beginning with the usual emergency services such as fire and ambulance and ending with such groups as the W.R.V.S., Red Cross and other voluntary bodies likely to be involved in first aid or the organisation of rest centres. If the status of the alert continued to escalate, there would be public warnings by police loudspeaker two hours before danger time.

It is the moment of decision on giving a public warning—a police responsibility—which calls for a certain nicety of judgement. What would be least helpful to the emergency planners would be for everyone on Canvey to make a rush for the mainland. This is one reason why loudspeaker warnings, which can be more informative, are preferred to the evocative siren. Group Captain Bowen's plans depend largely on the wisdom of staying put. "We don't want them all to rush out," he says. "People are best off in their own houses." If evacuation were necessary, he would expect most people to look after themselves and find their way to the homes of families and friends, leaving the emergency services to cope with the disabled, aged and sick.

Inevitably, much of all this is speculative; a lot would depend, for example, on the time of day. And although the emergency services conduct frequent internal exercises, there is, as Group Captain Bowen says, "a limit to how far you can go by way of practice" as far as the general public is concerned. "For instance, it would be ridiculous to clear the whole of Canvey Island just as an exercise—people wouldn't stand for it." Arguments about the adequacy or otherwise of the precautions, he adds, will go on and on. "I don't say the scheme won't creak and groan a bit," he says, "but we have a more sophisticated machine than in 1953, and we're backed by emergency powers as far as we want to go."

The more widespread use of radio by the emergency services and also by such other authorities as county highways departments, water and electricity undertakings is one example Group Captain Bowen quotes of this increased sophistication. In 1953, it was the existence of its V.H.F. radio network that enabled the Eastern Electricity Board to marshal its manpower resources to the best advantage, and in addition, in some places, to summon other emergency help where telephone lines had failed. (Many lines had been put out of action in the twenty-four hours of gales that preceded the flood.) The communications network between authorities, too, is now easier to manage than in 1953. In Essex local government reorganisation has reduced the number of separate district authorities from thirty-four to fourteen. Similarly, reorganisation of the water authorities has consolidated the link between sea defence and river works, a link which had been established in 1953 but was still in the shakedown stage. The development of county social services departments

Survivors at a reception centre at Kings Lynn on Sunday manage thin smiles for the camera: except for the cat. *Press Association*

over the past twenty years has provided a corps of people to organise rest centres and cope with other evacuation problems, while the school meals service is a ready-made source of emergency feeding. From where Group Captain Bowen sits, it looks as if a flood would be uncomfortable and might well—especially along the less well-defended coastline in south Essex—result in considerable damage, but it should certainly give people more warning than in 1953 and so such a shattering death-toll should be avoided.

Like Essex, the Greater London Council, too, is anxious to keep people off the streets in the event of a flood. It has the advantage here in that bungalows are rare in the vulnerable areas. The G.L.C.'s advice to householders is that they should retreat on hearing the warning to an upper floor; but "before they go upstairs they should turn off their gas and electricity at the mains and collect some blankets, a torch, candles and matches, canned food, drinking water and a portable radio. People must stay where they are . . ."

But if you live in the intensely urban streets of, say, Fulham or Hammersmith, it is very difficult to translate these instructions into the possibility of action that might one day have to be taken. The war was different; for one thing, it was finite, and then again the danger was ever-present. Despite intensive publicity using all the media available, it is said that when the G.L.C. tested its warning sirens in 1974 half the population didn't hear them, and of those who did many did not know what they meant. Unless you are one of the very few people who were about in the early morning of 1st February 1953 and saw the Thames lapping at the top of the embankment parapets in Chelsea, Westminster and Blackfriars, floods would come way down on your list of city hazards. By contrast, memories of 1953 along the east coast are more compelling, and a large proportion of the population are weather-watchers either by habit or profession and are therefore more sensitive to the dangers. Suffolk's County Emergency Officer, Wing Commander D. C. Charlier, places a great deal of reliance on local wisdom when it comes to recognising imminent danger, and this is one of the reasons why decisions on warning the public to get upstairs or get out are left to the local police.

The warning system in Suffolk is in four stages. The lowest phase, "Flood alert", is issued about twelve hours before high water at Lowestoft and indicated only the *possibility* of a tide above danger level. About four hours before high water, the "Flood danger" warning goes out if the possibility has hardened into a *probability*, and at this stage the district authorities in coastal areas are informed. These two stages are a direct response to warnings from Bracknell, but from then on the Suffolk police take over the responsibility of issuing further warnings according to local conditions. The signal "Flood arouse" brings the emergency services to a state of readiness, with boats, equipment and road transport positioned, manpower called in to look after communications, outlying houses warned and police loudspeaker vans brought to standby. Finally, "Flood alarm" is the "this is it" signal. The police tour urban areas with loud hailers and whistles, rural beat constables telephone or visit isolated farms and cottages on their lists, and the support services likely to be needed in case of evacuation are put into gear.

Once the warning sequence has been gone through, responsibility—for evacuation, rescue and repairs—is channelled through the county emergency office. Each area in Suffolk has a local emergency committee which can provide some self-help for individual communities. By this stage, however, there would also be on hand the county's own road gangs, a trained force of some 400 men, lifeboat services, local boatmen, the W.R.V.S., Red Cross, St John Ambulance and other voluntary organisations, and the water authorities' local staff. The Suffolk plan even includes a provision for one of the niggling problems of 1953—providing an information service for worried relations from outside the flooded area enquiring about their families; this would be staffed by Town and Country Planning staff using county libraries and mobile library vans.

It must be said here that, given the thinness on the ground of county policemen, the proposal that, in scattered areas, householders should receive an individual warning of "Flood alarm" from the police seems more optimistic than realistic. However, everyone I have spoken to in the more remote areas of Suffolk and Norfolk seems well satisfied with the system and assures me that the procedure, so far from being a pious hope against a remote possibility, is carried out frequently according to purely local conditions. Lists of people to be called are revised each year before the danger season starts, and the warning routine seems by now to be well-established and foolproof.

As it happens, all these emergency arrangements were put to a severe test on the night of 3rd-4th January 1976. On Friday 2nd January, conditions in the North Sea were building up in a manner uncannily similar to that of 1953. A deepening depression had moved eastwards across Scotland on Friday 2nd January, with hurricane-force winds, and by the Friday night it was moving southwards from a position off eastern Scotland, sweeping down the North Sea in the classic surge-producing pattern. High tides were due on Saturday, reaching their predicted peak on the evening tide only half an hour later than the fateful tides of twenty-three years before. The winds, which had been south-westerly and westerly, backed to the north during Saturday, building up a surge and preventing the morning tide from getting away. By the afternoon of Saturday, 3rd January, it was beginning to look like a repeat performance of 1953.

The warning service did its duty. "Flood alert" and "Flood danger" warnings went out from Bracknell to the coastal authorities during Saturday morning and afternoon, and as the water level continued to rise the local emergency offices were mobilised. The log-book of the Suffolk emergency team tells a typical story.

It was at 8.45 on the Saturday evening that Suffolk police issued the "Flood alarm" signal. Forty-five minutes later, the county's emergency control centre in Ipswich was opened up, and a message was sent to recall members of the emergency team from a Home Office conference in Cambridge. At 9.37 p.m., the police reported that the flood level was two or three feet above danger point at Lowestoft, Southwold, Aldeburgh, Felixstowe and Ipswich. At 10.50 p.m. key officials of the education, highways and social services departments were alerted, and fifteen minutes later sandbags, traffic diversion signs and debris-moving equipment were ordered up. In his eleven years as Suffolk's emergency officer, Wing Commander Charlier was facing his first "Flood alarm". "This is it, we thought," he remembers, "and everyone was ready to go—the district controls were operating, the emergency centre was manned, all the services were organised."

But as high tide time at Ipswich approached—1.48 a.m. on the Sunday—the wind veered and dropped. At Lowestoft, water had come over the level of

The shopkeeper who coined this name for his self-service store (a new concept in the Britain of 1953) could hardly have guessed how literal it was to prove. In fact, the amount of reported looting after the flood was very small — the police, Army patrols and local vigilantes saw to that.
Walmsley and Webb

the esplanade to a depth of about two feet, and then stopped. There was some flooding and evacuation of houses at Reydon, near Southwold, at Beccles and Bungay, and at Wherstead near Ipswich. But with the change of wind the danger quickly subsided, and at 1.48 p.m. the emergency centre was able to stand down the emergency services and itself close down.

Evidence from a number of sources suggests that in 1976 the likelihood of severe flooding, given the predicted height of the tide and the atmospheric conditions which had been building up over the previous day, was in fact greater than could have been foreseen in 1953. There was, indeed, some damage. At Cleethorpes, some 400 houses were flooded to depths of up to four feet and the railway embankment gave way. There was overtopping of the sea walls at Mablethorpe and Sutton-on-Sea. At Walcott, in Norfolk, the concrete sea-wall rebuilt after 1953 gave way and about 150 people had to be evacuated from their homes. At Cley, Salthouse and Blakeney on the north Norfolk coast, about 200 people were evacuated and there was damage to beach-chalets and boat-houses.

But the contrast between 1976 and 1953 was marked. There was a helicopter standing by for the Walcott rescue, though it was not, in the event, needed; and when the north wall of Breydon Water, behind Great Yarmouth, collapsed in three places there was a helicopter on hand to ferry in 8,000 sandbags to plug the gaps. In 1953 when the banks of Breydon Water were breached "the earliest repair works", a river board report later noted, "were carried out by rowing sand-filled bags out over the marshes to the breaches in scores of small boats". In Suffolk, rest centres were being prepared long before crisis point was reached. The evidence is that the Sunday newspaper report which asked the front page question, in the true traditions of instant journalism, "Could we have had more warning of the peril?" was whistling hopefully in the dark. The national warning system had worked according to plan. Reserves of manpower and equipment had been called up to breaches, actual and potential. No one died. Suffolk's Emergency Plans Officer declared himself well-satisfied with the exercise, apart from a few small details. In its first test for real, the system inaugurated after 1953 had vindicated itself. But it is well not to be too complacent; in 1953 the Dutch national warning system had been in existence for nearly forty years, and had been tried and tested many times, but it could not prevent nearly 1,800 deaths and the loss of some 50,000 head of cattle when "more than fifty dykes burst almost simultaneously and nearly half a million acres of polder country were swallowed by the raging sea".

The 1976 threat was, at all events, alarming enough to create its own mythology, like the survival-dedicated pigs of 1953: a story was circulating on the night of the surge that 600 people had gathered on the front at Felixstowe and were urging the sea to go back. Perhaps it is worth noting another similarity with 1953 in the number of newspaper stories placed during the following week by the public relations departments of insurance companies and institutions explaining why people who had been flooded out, and had thought themselves covered, wouldn't be getting adequate compensation after all, although, obscurely, premiums would of course have to be raised.

And what of the sea-defences? In 1953 these had suffered, as was mentioned in Chapter One, from neglect and positive damage during the war years which had never been put right. They suffered also from the division of

In repairing the sea defences, time was of the essence, and the work carried on by floodlight. For many National Servicemen, it was a welcome relief from the barrack square. National Service provided a reserve of labour that would not be available in similar circustances today.

Walmsley and Webb

A concave "wave wall" of the kind built since 1953 at a number of vulnerable points on the East Coast. The curve defeats the scouring action which does so much damage when the seas are heavy. The effectiveness of the concave wall has been proven – but most of the coastline is still protected by shingle or clay banks, or by "step" concrete walls which are very susceptible to damage. *The Author*

responsibility until 1952 among a number of small authorities which were constrained both by the difficulties of administering small units of what is, after all, a highly technical service and by the limitations on their power to raise a rate.

It was perhaps hard luck on the newly-constituted river boards of 1952 that, so soon in their lives, they had to face the problems created by a major disaster; but they did so largely by carrying on the traditions that had gone before. Thus, "poor" areas which had made do with clay banks of indifferent construction continued to do so, while areas where the tradition ran to concrete facings saw this form of protection restored. In 1953, there were along the east coast a few short stretches of concave "wave walls", designed to absorb and throw back the force of the sea. Almost without exception these held; but while damaged sections of this form of defence were restored, there was little extension of it to other vulnerable areas. At the same time, stepped concrete walls which had proved especially sensitive to wave action were replaced with more of the same.

This is not to say that there were no improvements after 1953. After 15,000,000 sandbags had been used as temporary stoppers, the coastal authorities conducted a step-by-step survey of the defences, the study of those stretches which had not given way being as important as the attempts to determine the reason for the breaches. To take one river board area as an example, in Norfolk and Suffolk clay walls were made one foot higher and one foot wider on the crest, given a 2:1 back slope to reduce the scouring effect of waves coming over, and widened at the base. At Sea Palling, the scene of Florence Ridley's agonies described earlier, a reinforced concrete wall was built and groynes were installed to help build up the depleted beach. Marram grass was planted to protect what remained of the sand-dunes behind the new wall. Altogether, over £1 million was spent on the eight-mile stretch between Happisburgh and Winterton, on Norfolk's vulnerable north-eastern tip. New sea walls and groynes were also constructed at Kessingland, Aldeburgh and Southtown, Great Yarmouth.

Official opinion, from both water and local authorities, is thus that sea-defences are now much more secure than in 1953. There remain, however, long stretches of "soft sea-defences" — sand-dunes or clay banks — and there is concern in some areas that these have not been maintained as carefully as they should be — concern reawakened to some extent by the comparatively slight overtopping in January 1976. Residents at Wells, for example, claim that the defences are no higher than in 1953, and at the time of writing were trying to put pressure on the Anglian Water Authority to build them up. At nearby Salthouse, flooded in the January 1976 surge, a £300,000 new flood bank is planned, and perhaps this has been a stimulus to the Wells concern. A few miles along the coast at Burnham Overy Staithe, however, there are disturbing reports of the erosion of the dunes which constitute the first line of defence. Sara Sproule, who lives in Burnham Norton and has known this stretch of coast for nearly thirty years, says: "It's quite alarming, the difference in the bit of beach to the east of the River Burn. Once, you could walk along the beach there at high tide, but not now. The waves break right up against the crumbling sandhills."

"What's happened is that the creek is being blocked up at the harbour," she goes on. "The River Burn now reaches the sea directly below the biggest of the sandhills, and that's where the biggest pressure is on the land. I think the possibility of it all happening again is coming on us faster and faster." The "creep" of shingle and sand at this point is unrestrained by groynes. And yet when I looked at this particular stretch of coast from Peter Hancock's farm gate, nothing could have seemed more secure.

Phenomenal surges like that of 1953 apart, erosion continues steadily, as on these dunes near Winterton. Every collapse — and there are many each winter — increases the vulnerability of the land behind. *The Author*

To the west of the river mouth, between Overy West Point and Scolt Head, a distance of about two miles, Sara Sproule has noticed, from her windows in Burnham Norton, an alarming increase over the past few years in her view of the sea. Not many years ago, it was hidden from view by the line of dunes, with only one small gap where the sea came through in 1953 and subsequently an attempt has been made to fill the gap by building up the sand again on a netting fence. But erosion has continued and now, she says, "you can see the breakers at high tide along almost the entire length between West Point and Scolt Head".

It has to be said, of course, that all stretches of sandy coastline are subject to constant change unless protected by groynes. Nevertheless, one cannot help wondering why this expedient has not been adopted along this stretch. Whatever the reason, and whatever the facts about the present state of the defences compared with 1953, the evidence of local day-by-day observations is, to say the least, disquieting.

It was disturbing, too, to find in December 1976 that at Waxham, near Sea Palling, the concave wave wall built as part of the post-1953 sea defence scheme — the most useful but most expensive form of defence, according to expert opinion — was almost completely covered with loose sand which would, in the event of a storm-driven high tide, render it ineffective. This is, incidentally, a popular spot for beach anglers, and the access path from the public road to the beach gave ample evidence of the effect of even relatively modest foot traffic on the endurance of the dunes.

Another Norfolk resident who is sceptical about what he calls the "standard blindfold of officials and experts" is Walter Powell, who lives near Winterton. He is particularly concerned with official neglect, and in some cases destruction, of the marrams — the sea-grass-covered dunes which, Mr Powell says, are the only reliable form of sea defence. Concrete walls and sandbags, he adds, are in his view little more than temporary expedients.

"Few people nowadays realise," says Mr Powell, "what vast, delicate and vulnerable structures the marrams are — and yet, once established and left entirely to nature, they would go on doing their work for literally centuries with no labour or expense in upkeep. They are now taken for granted and have so far survived only because, until recently, they have not been seriously abused except at holiday resorts such as Sea Palling and Hemsby. Now, however, with the huge increase of permanent residents and the greater influx of holiday visitors, the whole coastline is endangered. Although marram grass seems indestructibly tough, when it is walked bare it is very reluctant indeed to regenerate."

But according to Mr Powell, the threat to the marrams does not come only from casual visitors: "Some ten years ago," he told me, "the Nature Conservancy (for some reason not apparent to me) bulldozed flat about two

The effectiveness of the concave wave wall is lost if sand is allowed to over-run it. This stretch of wall on the north Norfolk coast was photographed in December 1976, just before the period of greatest danger of a recurrence of the floods of 1953. *The Author*

acres of the Winterton dunes and the flattened area was then planted with tufts of marram grass. This same place remains bare to this day (1976), despite the fact that it had been fenced off all of that time. A generation ago, this nature reserve was deep in marrams and other grasses, heather, mosses and prostrate willow, and the whole area was being steadily colonised by scrub birch, alder, rhododendrons, elder, oaks and many other plants which were forming a natural backing of immense strength and tenacity to the dunes." Where the official tractors have spared this complex structure, says Mr Powell, it is steadily being demolished by such activities as pony-trekking, motor-cycle scrambling and indiscriminate rambling. Added to all this have been the effects of two years—1975 and 1976—of exceptionally damaging and wide-spread heathland fires. "Tiny footpaths have become wide sandy tracks," Mr Powell reports, "grass has been scorched threadbare and what were great stretches of heather and young trees are now blackened and dead." Only complete closure of the area to the public so that regeneration can proceed undisturbed can, Mr Powell believes, restore the sea defences at this point.

I confess that when I first heard from Mr Powell I thought that he was overstating his case—until I went to look at the Winterton dunes for myself. True enough, they are a sorry sight. The network of paths crossing them has merged almost to the point of uniform baldness; there is little enough cover to resist the slightest breeze, leave alone the effect of seas driven by a northerly gale. When I was there, in midwinter, they still carried the scars of the summer's traffic—and indeed the traffic continues to some extent all the year round: as I was leaving, two horses arrived—in horse-boxes, so evidently from some distance—for what was clearly their daily exercise. Although not developed to the extent of, say, Hemsby or even Sea Palling, Winterton is a popular spot in the summer, and indeed there is a fair-sized car park adjacent

The road to the sea at Sea Palling, where the surge broke through on the night of 31st January 1953. The sea defences have been considerably raised and strengthened at this point—but to allow new building so close to the dunes looks like tempting Providence. *The Author*

to the dunes to cater for visitors. I could not help comparing the state of the dunes there with those at Scolt Head, near Burnham Norton, which are not accessible by road and are walked only by those provident enough to take a boat from Brancaster Staithe or hardy enough to reach them on foot across the marshes. At Scolt, the marrams have built up just such a complex of vegetation as Mr Powell describes, and indeed one dare not stray far from the narrow paths because of the razor-like propensities of some of the species. Similarly, at Holkham, a couple of miles away, the structure of the dunes has been maintained, though in this case allowing for the admission of some car-borne tourists. Duckboards have been laid over some of the more vulnerable stretches of dune, with notices urging visitors to keep to them, and the number of visitors has been kept down by charging a relatively high price for parking at the one spot from which the dunes are accessible. This may well have to be the answer for villages close to the dunes along the east coast; car parks in aid of village funds, as at Sea Palling, Winterton and a number of other places, are all very well, but the true price may well be the very security of those communities themselves.

On the question of preventing further disasters by better sea-defences, the Waverley Report of 1954 was hard but realistic. After explaining that the protection of human life must depend upon an efficient warning system, it went on: "In considering the margin of safety for sea-defences, we have . . . had the protection of property mainly in mind. If there could have been a combination of all the known adverse factors, the water level reached in January 1953 would have been considerably higher, possibly by several feet, than it in fact was. The cost of affording protection against the worst possibilities would be colossal, and we have ruled out any idea of being able to recommend measures designed to secure complete protection against every conceivable element of tide and surge. Even the cost of protecting the whole coast against conditions like those of January last year would be prohibitive. To what then must the standard of defence be related? The natural and indeed inevitable course in these circumstances is to relate the standard of defence to the character and amount of the property to be protected."

In this connection, Lord Waverley—the chairman of the committee that produced the Report—had some apposite things to say when, in December 1953, he spoke to the Institution of Civil Engineers' post-mortem on the disaster, and his remarks indicate how far away from certainties any discussion of future possibilities must be. He and his committee, he said, had concluded quite clearly that "further investigations and research was required in several directions before it could be said that they had acquired all the information necessary for the effective planning of coastal defences. They knew what had happened in January. They knew what the effects of the surge . . . and the high winds at that time had been on various types of coastal defence; but they did not know, he thought, as much as they should about the possibility of attack . . . under different conditions and different states of the wind and tide, and it was in regard to these matters that they hoped that further research might be undertaken".

The Waverley Report itself drew attention in another passage to an aspect of the flood damage of 1953 which seems, in the eyes of any observer of the east coast today, subsequently to have been ignored. "We have been impressed,"

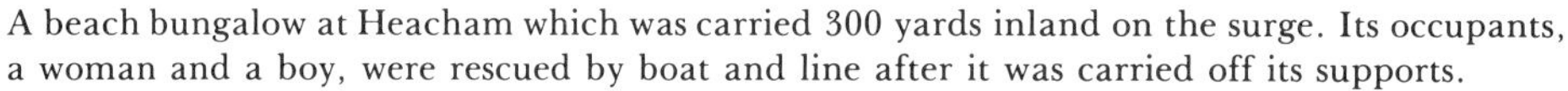
A beach bungalow at Heacham which was carried 300 yards inland on the surge. Its occupants, a woman and a boy, were rescued by boat and line after it was carried off its supports.

The Life Boat Inn at Sea Palling, Norfolk. The original inn was demolished after the 1953 floods – in which the licensee lost his life – and the new building carries a plaque recording the disaster. In one of the bars is an impression by a local artist of the night of the flood. Yet the new building is only yards from a high-water mark, and below the level of the sea-wall. Nearby, seen to the left of the picture, is a row of newly-built shops with flats above. *The Author*

the Report said, "by the fact that much of the damage done by the 1953 floods was the result of sporadic and ill-considered development near the coast which has led to unnecessary expense both by way of payments from the Lord Mayor's Fund and by way of additional expenditure on restoration and improvement works. The machinery for preventing such development already exists under the Town and Country Planning Act 1947. We think that all possible steps should be taken to prevent further undesirable development and that full use of the machinery of the Planning Act should be made. We understand that local planning authorities generally consult river boards on suggestions for development which may involve draining considerations, including flooding. *We must stress the importance of such consultations.*" (The italics are mine.)

I am assured that this consultation now regularly takes place, and indeed I have seen copies of enquiries to the river divisions on the suitability of certain coastal developments. But plans nevertheless have a way of slipping through, especially when other considerations, such as the amount of local employment offered by a holiday camp or a caravan site in an area dependent partially upon tourism and partially upon the demand for agricultural labour, which is declining, are involved. Whether or not planning authorities are more careful in future, the huge caravan site at Snettisham Beach, literally in the lee of the inner flood bank and well below the level which was overtopped in 1953, and the holiday chalet town at Hemsby, some miles to the east, are only two examples which show that the important paragraph quoted above from Waverley was forgotten after 1953. It is to be hoped that it will be remembered in future when commercial pressures, such as those applied in 1976 for sanction for a huge holiday complex at Sea Palling, are brought to bear on planning authorities.

The development of caravan sites, holiday flatlets, and chalet camps is, of course, highly profitable, but it is, in truth, unlikely that they bring much economic benefit to their local communities, whatever arguments might be put forward in planning applications. In so far as caravanners and chalet holidaymakers buy locally, they tend to buy from on-site shops; but more frequently they arrive with car-loads of food bought at the cut prices available in Midlands supermarkets. Undoubtedly, however, the arguments in favour of tourist development are attractive to the authorities in an area like East Anglia where farming is in decline as an employer of labour and where the search must be on for new focal points in the regional economy. The county authorities, in fact, have to face the same dilemma as the villagers of Sea Palling, who collect car parking fees in aid of village pensioners—the problem of deciding when enough is enough.

Not all the concern about the development of the north Norfolk coast, however, is related to large-scale development. Walter Powell, quoted earlier in connection with the Winterton sea-defences, mentioned to me the number of "holiday" bungalows on this coast which were in fact used all the year round, in some cases despite the lack of approach roads or sewerage facilities. Checking during the bleak midwinter of 1976-77, I found that this was true enough: at Snettisham Beach, at South Beach, Hunstanton, at Eccles, Sea Palling and Winterton, there were plenty of properties in the lee of the dunes or the sea-walls—some of them clearly built since 1953—which were in permanent occupation. At South Beach, Hunstanton, some new blocks of maisonettes were being put up. At Eccles and Sea Palling, gaps in the rows of wooden chalets, presumably left by the surge of 1953, had been filled with

Caravan site at Heacham Beach, near Hunstanton. Pictured in midwinter, the site was deserted, which was just as well since the caravans were well below the level of the shingle bank.
The Author

New development at South Hunstanton, literally "across the road" from the sea-wall. This is an area which suffered heavily — in both damage and loss of life — in 1953. At Christmas 1976, when this picture was taken, many of the houses in this road seemed fully occupied.
The Author

new, brick-built houses. Of course, it is difficult to see how, even if planning permission is granted subject to summer holiday use only, the restriction can be enforced once a property is built. Perhaps the only answer is a policy of gradually running down these vulnerable communities as the older wooden buildings decay.

Alternatively, there is perhaps a case for making the ownership of such properties a less attractive proposition — possibly by surcharging owners for sea-defences, or demanding that they should be insured fully and that local authorities should be indemnified against claims for flood damage on public funds. This would at least prevent any of the resources of such funds as the Lord Mayor of London's 1953 collection, provided largely by voluntary effort, from being diverted from cases of genuine need into compensation for traders; or from the taxpayer's having to recompense from public funds developers who should have calculated the true risks of their business ventures before they started.

There remains the question of what local people can do for themselves to protect and strengthen sea-defences. While, in theory, the removal of responsibility for sea defence from local hands should have led to an overall improvement in standards, and has clearly done so along some stretches of the coast where the Sea Breach Commissioners were either lackadaisical or hard up, the effect has been to transfer responsibility to a mysterious "them" — the river divisions of the huge Anglian Water Authority whose headquarters, miles away in Huntingdon, may well have other problems on its mind. The element of local self-help which once characterised sea defence work has thus disappeared — possibly, but not certainly, for the better. Along the Lincolnshire coast at South Killingholme, for example, local landowners used to arrange for slag to be deposited along the seaward side of the clay bank each autumn. Their neighbours at Wood Farm Bank, near Grimsby, used lump chalk, distributed from barges at the rate of some 200 tons per mile — less effective than slag, since it tended to break up, but better than nothing. And Florence Ridley remembers that in the Sea Palling area "years ago the local farmers used to trim their hedges and lay the pieces on the sea side of the hills, and in this way the sand was caught and held, forming a barrier. It's years since this practice was followed, and the farmers did not help when they ploughed down their hedges for cheapness". She notes, too, that some owners of holiday chalets behind the sand-dunes "began to hack away at the hills to make gardens, weakening the already weak hills". Even at Scolt Head, a nature reserve unrestrictedly open to the public but with no road access, there is concern about damage done to the dunes—savagely cut back by the 1953 surge—by the feet of increasing numbers of visitors.

But although more care might slightly reduce local risks, it must remain a fact of life for those who live along the east coast that they live in the shadow of the sea. Three times since 1953, there have been comparable surges. As the interim report of the Waverley Committee put it in July 1953: "We have no evidence to show that there is any periodicity in the occurrence of such a combination of phenomena (as wind plus surge plus tide). A combination of surge and tide such as that of 31st January-1st February 1953 may not occur for many years, but it may occur next winter. We should also point out that, given the same distribution and sequence of winds and atmospheric pressure the disaster would have been worse if . . . the time of the maximum surge had been nearer to that of high water of the ordinary tide; or . . . the height of the ordinary tide had been as great as it was both a fortnight earlier and a fortnight later; or . . . there had been much more fresh water coming down the rivers."

Figures published in the Waverley Report backed up the view that the frequency of high tides along the east coast is increasing. Between 1820 and 1839 high tides at Sheerness or Southend reached eleven feet above Ordnance Datum (Newlyn)—that is, "sea level" to laymen—on six occasions, above twelve feet on one occasion, and not at all above thirteen feet. Between 1877 and 1896 the relative figures were fifteen, one and nil. Between 1934 and 1953 they were thirty-nine, nine and four. Such statistics must suggest that the gradual sinking of the English coast towards the south-east has come out of the geologist's notebook into the realms of practical reality.

But this is a case in which statistics are not everything, and, because each breakthrough of the sea is an individual case, indeed may be worth very little. In a paper given to the Institution of Civil Engineers in December 1953, naval oceanographer Commander W. I. Farquharson discussed the variables that must be brought into consideration in assessing future possibilities of a recurrence of 1953. "There are no known reasons," he said, "why combinations of surge and tide more adverse than any hitherto recorded should not occur in the future."

The factors involved were, he went on, three in number. First was the force and duration of the northerly winds which have generated the surge and which built up its elevation. Second was the height to which the tide is predicted to rise. Third was the *interval* between the arrival of the crest of the surge and high water of the tide. If the height was high and the interval was short, then even a small surge could be dangerous. If the surge had a very great elevation and the interval between surge and high tide was short, there was a dangerous situation even at neap tides. If the strong northerly winds were prolonged, then the surge might have a high elevation for so long a period that a dangerous level might be reached at high tide even if the interval between surge and tide were long.

Putting it another way, there are an infinite number of permutations between wind, surge and tide in the North Sea, some of which could bring disaster on the 1953 scale no matter what improvements have been made to the sea-defences. The message cannot be escaped: sooner or later, the sea will come in again to the low lands of the east coast, though thanks to the warning system it should not again—provided the system is kept in good order—take such a toll of human life. But for those who live on the coast, the price of the bracing air, the clear skies and the freedom from city pressures must always be eternal vigilance.

Could it happen again? *Press Association*

Acknowledgements

MY MAIN source for this book has been the reminiscences of people who were directly involved in the 1953 floods. Where I have quoted directly from my correspondents and contacts, they are acknowledged in the text. I have also made use of some quotations from interviews given to local newspapers, and these are acknowledged chapter by chapter in the list that follows.

I would particularly like to thank Florence Ridley of Stalham, formerly of Sea Palling, and Christopher Manser of Southend, formerly of Canvey Island, for letting me have such detailed accounts of their experiences in 1953, whose recall must have been especially painful. I must also thank the countless other residents and former residents of East Anglia who got in touch with me following local press inquiries who are not quoted directly in the text but whose help filled in much background detail and made available valuable material. I am indebted in particular to Mrs L. M. Barton (Felixstowe), Mrs Jill David (London), H. W. Durrant (Ipswich), Frank Green (Cromer), Mrs M. Lenton (Andover), Mrs R. Mason (Colchester), Mrs H. M. Playford (Wisbech), Mrs L. C. Radford (Haynford) and Barry Turner (London).

My thanks are also due to the Anglian Water Authority (Norfolk and Suffolk River Division and Lincolnshire River Division), the Chartered Insurance Institute, the *Dovercourt Standard*, the *East Anglian Daily Times*, the *Eastern Daily Press*, East Midland Allied Press, Essex County Council (Emergency Plans Office), Essex County Library, the *Felixstowe Times*, Lincolnshire County Council, the Meteorological Office Library, Norfolk County Library (Norfolk Local Studies Library), Norfolk Record Office, the Norwich Union Insurance Group, the *Southend Evening Echo*, Suffolk County Council (Emergency Plans Team), Suffolk County Library, and Mr I. H. Whitworth of the Holkham Estate Office.

For background information on the disaster, I am indebted to the *Report of the Departmental Committee on Coastal Flooding* (The Waverley Report), H.M.S.O. 1954, and to *The Great Tide: the story of the great flood disaster in Essex 1953*, by Hilda Grieve, Essex County Council 1959.

I am indebted to several individuals and organisations for help in obtaining illustrations. I would ask that the credit under the photographs be taken as an acknowledgement both of copyright and of help received. In addition I would like to thank Mr Henry Clarke and Mr Alden for their help and guidance.

Finally, my special thanks to Sara Sproule of Burnham Norton, in whose house this book was largely written.

Chapter One

The quotation on the Hickling flood of 1287 is from John of Oxnead, and, with the Horsey resident's strictures on the Sea Breach Commissioners, is taken from a booklet published by the East Suffolk and Norfolk River Board in June 1959 to mark the completion of new sea-defences between Happisburgh and Winterton. The quotation on the predictability of tidal oscillations is from G. Reynolds, "Storm surge research", *Weather*, April 1953. Letters critical of the closure of Airmet appeared in *Weather*, March 1953. The Ministry of Agriculture report quoted on the lack of warning for farmers is R. B. Ferro *et al*, "County reports of the East Coast sea floods", *Agriculture* 60, 1953. Eye-witnesses' reports from Holland are from H. A. Q. v. Ufford, "The disastrous storm surge of 1 February", *Weather*, April 1953. The quotation on conditions in the North Sea on the afternoon of 31st January is from J. R. Rossiter, "The North Sea storm surge of 31 January and 1 February", *Philosophical Transactions of the Royal Society 1954*. (Incidentally, all estimates of the height of the surge are speculative, since every tide gauge on the east coast was put out of action by the surge itself.) The commentator on the holding-up of the previous ebb tide is H. A. P. Jensen, "Tidal inundations past and present, Part I", *Weather*, March 1953, who is also the source of the quotation on the overtopping of the banks.

Chapter Two

The opening quotation is from J. V. Spalding, "A general survey of the damage done and action taken", *Institution of Civil Engineers' Conference on the North Sea floods*, December 1953. The comment by the Norfolk County Planning Officer on the disaster south of Hunstanton is from Norfolk County Council, *The Flood Disaster 31 January—1 February 1953*, N.C.C. County Planning Office, December 1953. The story of the trapped train appeared in "British Railways and the January Floods", *The Railway Magazine*, May 1953, and the account of flooding at Salthouse by Margaret Cooke was printed in *The Daily Telegraph*, 2nd February 1953. The quotation on the hidden extent of the floods is from J. V. Spalding, *op. cit.* The story of the Lowestoft Choral Society's annual dinner appeared in "East Coast flood 1953", *East Anglian Daily Times*, 31st January 1973.

Chapter Three

The stories of the Sorick family of Southwold, the Southwold ambulance, Jimmy Thompson of Halesworth, Alan Aldridge of Aldeburgh, the R.A.F. guard at Orfordness and the quotation from Arthur Simpson on the evacuation of Jaywick are from the *East Anglian Daily Times, op. cit.* The story of the

Lee-over-Sands holiday camp manager is from Grieve, *op. cit.* The Langer Road, Felixstowe casualty list and some of the stories of survivors from the Langer Road area are from the *Felixstowe Times*, 6th February 1953. In the interests of her surviving relatives, "Mrs Crawford" is a fictitious name.

Chapter Four

Information on damage to electricity supplies is from *The East Coast floods of 1953: the restoration of electricity supplies*, Eastern Electricity Board 1954. Information on the aftermath of the disaster at Felixstowe came from the *Felixstowe Times* and the *East Anglian Daily Times, op. cit.* Information on Foulness and on the reluctant head teacher is from Grieve, *op. cit.* The quotation on conditions in the East Riding of Yorkshire is from R. B. Ferro *et al, op. cit.* The quotations from engineers' reports on the Lincolnshire sea defences are from documents in the possession of the Anglian Water Authority (Lincolnshire River Division).

Chapter Five

The insurance journal quoted is *The Insurance Mail,* 15th April 1953 (but, of course, the comments on insurance other than this direct quotation are my own). Edward Sillett and Charles Goodey are quoted from the *East Anglian Daily Times, op. cit.*, which is also the source of the story about Anne Smith of Shottisham. The difficulties of the Harwich pensioner over tobacco tokens appeared in the *Harwich and Dovercourt Standard,* 13th February 1953. Mrs A. M. Vincent's interview with the reporter appeared in the *Harwich and Dovercourt Standard,* September 4th 1953. The quotation about the camp owned by Shell which might be used for temporary housing is from Grieve, *op. cit.*

Chapter Six

The G.L.C.'s advice to householders is quoted from a 1976 press release. Detail on the 1976 floods in Suffolk is from "A Report on the activation of the County Emergency Organisation during the storm tide crisis of 3-4 January 1976", Suffolk County Council Emergency Plans Team, 1976. The quotation on the situation in Holland is from H. A. Q. v. Ufford, *op. cit.* Information on repair measures by the East Suffolk and Norfolk River Board is from the Board's *Annual Report,* 1953. Lord Waverley's speech is quoted from the *Institution of Civil Engineers' Conference on the North Sea floods, op. cit.*, and Commander Farquharson's comments on future possibilities of flooding are from the same source.

Index

A

Aberfan disaster, 99, 107
Admiralty, 24, 28
Agriculture and Fisheries, Ministry of, 25, 96, 103
Airmet service, 24
Aldeburgh, 54-55, 87, 116, 120
Alexandra Hotel, Dovercourt, 60
Alford, 91
Anglian Water Authority, 112, 120, 127
Australia, relief from, 89
Azores, 19

B

Bacton, 38
Barking, 12, 110
Barra Head, 20
Bathside, Harwich, 58, 59, 90, 102
Bawdsey, 51, 87
Beccles, 117
Belfast Lough, 20
Belgium, flood damage, 27
Benfleet, 66, 71, 73
Bentwaters, USAF, 8, 52
Blackfriars, 115
Blakeney, 36, 75, 117
Blyth, River, 51
Bracknell (Meteorological Office H.Q.), 109, 112, 115
Bramble Island, 62, 91
Brancaster Staithe, 123
Breydon Water, 40-41, 87, 117
Brightlingsea, 11
British Broadcasting Corporation, 19, 22, 24, 54, 61, 78-79, 82
British Railways, 22
Broads, the, 15, 41
Bungay, 117
Burn, River, 32, 120
Burnham Market, 76
Burnham Norton, 13, 32, 79, 120, 121, 123
Burnham Overy, 14, 30
Burnham Overy Staithe, 120

C

Caister, 11
Cambridge, 116
Canada, relief from, 89
Canvey Island, 15, 25, 27, 44, 52, 65-68, 69, 70, 71, 81, 89, 95, 97, 98, 103, 104, 112, 113
Cavendish Hotel, Felixstowe, 56, 82, 93
Chancellor of the Exchequer, 99
Chat Moss, 16
Chelmsford, 79, 112
Chelsea, 69, 115
Chiswick, 110
Churchill, Sir Winston, 99, 106
Civil Defence, 71, 95, 104, 105, 110, 111
Civil Engineers, Institution of, 124, 128
Clacton, 38, 62, 95, 103, 105
Cleethorpes, 28, 70, 117
Cley, 36, 70, 74-75, 87, 103, 117
Commons, House of, 93, 94, 96, 98, 99, 107
Costa Hill, 20
Cromer, 11

D

Deal, 70
Deben, River, 51
Deepdale Marsh, 13, 14, 32
Dereham, 87
Diamond Street, Kings Lynn, 49
Dock Lane, Bramble Island, 62
Dovercourt, 9, 58, 61, 62, 90, 102
Dovercourt Sailing Club, 62
Dunstable (former Meteorological Office H.Q.), 8, 19, 20
Dunwich, 12, 53

E

East Anglian Daily Times, 104
East End, London, 110
East Riding, Yorkshire, 83
East Suffolk and Norfolk River Board, 84, 85
Eastern Electricity Board, 51, 53, 79-80, 90, 91, 113
Eccles, 126

F

Felixstowe, 27, 44, 51, 55, 56, 78, 81, 84, 93, 95, 96, 105, 116, 118
Ferry Road, Southwold, 52, 53

Fleetwood, 20
Foulness Island, 70, 81, 95, 103
Freeman Street, Wells, 30-31
Frinton, 61
Fulham, 114

G
Gas Works Cottages, Felixstowe, 57
Great Ouse, 14, 27
Great Yarmouth, 15, 25, 28, 40, 44, 49, 70, 80, 84, 88, 91, 95, 102, 117, 120
Greater London Council, 110, 114, 115
Grimsby, 29, 127
Guava, trawler, 42-44

H
Halesworth, 51
Hammersmith, 114
Happisburgh, 11, 15, 39, 120
Harwich, 9, 16, 22, 58, 59-61, 62, 90, 91, 94, 95, 96, 102, 103, 105
Harwich and Dovercourt Standard, 102, 103
Heacham, 36, 75, 103
Hebrides, 20
Hemsby, 87, 121, 122, 125
Hickling, 12
High Street, Benfleet, 66
Holkham, 13, 32, 44, 49, 76, 77, 83, 103, 106, 123
Holland, 22-23, 25-26, 27, 44, 51, 69, 118
Holme, 103
Home Office, 110, 116
Home Secretary, 93, 98
Horsey, 16
Housing and Local Government, Ministry of, 79, 96
Hunstanton, 14, 32, 34, 36, 44, 46-47, 70, 75, 84, 85, 87, 95, 103, 105, 126
Huntingdon, 127

I
Immingham Dock, 25
Ipswich, 79, 82, 102, 116, 117
Irish Sea, 20, 22

J
Jaywick, 27, 38, 44, 52, 62-64, 65, 103

K
Kessingland, 120
Kings Lynn, 25, 27, 30, 32, 33, 34, 44, 46, 49, 51, 70, 75, 91, 103, 105
Kinloss, RAF, 20

L
Landguard Road, Felixstowe, 81
Langer Road, Felixstowe, 55, 57, 81
Langton Hills, 97
Larne, 20
Lee-over-sands, 64
Lichfield Road, Great Yarmouth, 40, 80-81
Life Boat Inn, Sea Palling, 39
Lincoln, 79
Loch Ryan, 20
London Bridge, 15, 25
London Electricity Board, 91
London Road, Lowestoft, 42
London Transport, 22
Lord Mayor of London's Flood Relief Fund, 98-99, 106, 125, 127
Louth, 91
Lowestoft, 8, 41-44, 45, 105, 116
Lynmouth, 107

M
Mablethorpe, 28, 32, 44, 70, 91, 104, 117
Manor Road, Dovercourt, 58, 61
Marsh Farm, Burnham Norton, 32, 37
Marsh House Farm, Burnham Overy, 30, 31
Maxwell Fyfe, Sir David, 93
Meals, near Wells, 32
Meteorological Office, 8, 19, 22, 24, 25, 28, 109, 112, 115
Michael Griffith, trawler, 20
Milleur Point, 20, 22
Model Farm, Holkham, 77

N
National Assistance Board, 96, 99
National Service, 84, 105, 112
Netherlands, *see* Holland
Newbridge House, Snettisham, 33
Newhaven, 22
Newlyn, 128
Norfolk Flood Relief Fund, 102
North Bay, Scarborough, 28
Norton Bank, 32
Norton Marsh, 13, 14, 32
Norway, 11, 20
Norwich, 79

O
Old Farm, Salthouse, 38
Olympia, 89
Ore, River, 51
Orfordness, 51, 55
Orford Road, Felixstowe, 55
Orkneys, 20
Orwell, River, 55, 57
Overy Staithe Bank, 31, 32
Overy West Point, 121

P
Partington, Mrs, 30
Point Clear Bay, 64
Postmaster-General, 24
Post Office, 80
Princess Victoria, British Railways ferry, 20, 22, 78-79

Q
Queen, Her Majesty the, 79
Queen Mary, Cunard liner, 22

R
Radio Luxembourg, 24
Rannoch Moor, 16
Red Cow, Canvey Island, 73
Red Cross, 49, 53, 62, 82, 105, 113, 115
Regent Cinema, Dovercourt, 102
Reydon, 52, 117
Richmond, Surrey, 110
Ritz Cinema, Felixstowe, 56
Rotary Clubs, 89, 93
Round Table, 89
Royal Air Force, 49, 51, 55, 70, 82
Royal Hotel, Lowestoft, 41
Royal Navy, 19, 45, 60
Rushden, 91

S
St Elizabeth's Flood, 1421, 15
St John Ambulance Brigade, 62, 73, 82, 94, 105, 115
St John's Church, Lowestoft, 41-42
Saddlebow Road, Kings Lynn, 36
Salthouse, 38, 70, 103, 117
Salvation Army, 82, 94
Samos, 88
Sandringham, 33
Scarborough, 28
Scolt Head, 13, 121, 123, 128
Scotland, 11, 20, 26, 109, 116
Scouts, 94
Scripture Gift Mission, 93
Sculthorpe, USAF, 47
Sea Breach Commissioners, 15-16, 127
Sea Palling, 8, 39-40, 48, 49-50, 69, 77, 87, 88, 93, 95, 105, 119, 121, 122, 123, 126, 127
Shell Petroleum Company, 97
Sheerness, 128
Shipden, 11
Ship Inn, Bacton, 38
Shottisham, 100
Shotley, 60
Sidmouth, 30
Sizewell, 51
Skegness, 70
Southampton, 22
South Beach, Hunstanton, 46-47, 75-76, 126
Snettisham, 32-36, 38, 45, 46, 49, 69, 75, 85, 95, 103, 105, 125, 126
Southend, 16, 82, 89, 128
South Killingholme, 127
South Lynn, Kings Lynn, 49
Southtown, Great Yarmouth, 120
Southwold, 51-52, 53, 77, 116, 117
Spurn Head, 28
Stalham, 88

Station Inn, Snettisham, 34
Stour Avenue, Felixstowe, 55
Stour, River, 57
Stranraer, 20
Suffolk Hotel, Lowestoft, 42
Surrey, 89
Survival (periodical), 111
Sutton-on-Sea, 32, 44, 70, 91, 103, 104, 117

T
Teddington, 15
Tees, River, 28
Thames, River, 15, 16, 26, 27, 65, 69, 70, 109, 110, 112, 115
Tilbury, 15
Times, The (London), 79
Townswomens' Guilds, 93
Trinity House, 9, 91
Twickenham, 110

INDEX

U

United States Air Force, 47, 49, 52, 82

V

Victoria Embankment, London, 69
Victoria Hotel, Holkham, 32

W

Walcott Gap, 38, 77, 117
Walton, 62
Walton-on-the-Naze, 12
Wash, the, 14, 27, 30, 32, 70
Waverley Committee, 24-26, 28, 123-125, 128
Waxham, 121
Weather Explorer, Ocean Weather Ship, 20
Wells, 13, 14, 28, 30-31, 32, 44, 76, 81, 87, 103, 106
Wenhaston, 52
Westminster, 115
Weybourne, 11
Wherstead, 117
Winter Garden Wall, Canvey Island, 73
Winterton, 120, 121, 122, 123, 126
Witton, 38
Womens' Institutes, 93
Womens' Royal Voluntary Service, 62, 71, 82, 93, 105, 113, 115
Wood Farm Bank, 127

Y

Yarmouth Mercury, 40
Yorkshire, relief from, 89

The situation at 06.00 hours on Saturday, 31st January 1953. Low Z is now moving round Scotland, and has deepened further. The forecast, issued at noon on Saturday, was that "all districts will have gale force winds, severe in many places, and squally showers, mainly of hail or snow".

Crown Copyright reserved. Reproduced with the permission of the Controller of Her Majesty's Stationery Office